THE RAPING OF AMERICA

By Scott Leddy

This book is not intended for the dead, undead or brain dead. Please stop reading if you are faint-at-heart, blind or display a cognitive inability to read or write. Please consult a physician before reviewing this book. Some patients analyzing the contents enclosed have exhibited signs of anxiety, vomiting, insomnia and high blood pressure, while others are prone to severe fits of rage. The following views are the expressed written thoughts of a demented author suffering long-term childhood trauma and mental anguish. Any written works with similar recorded views are purely coincidental. Most of the information contained within is sourced. The book's contents are the expressed written opinion of the author and don't necessarily reflect the views of said sources. If any of these sources desire their content immediately removed from the aforementioned publication then please notify the author via scott.leddy@yahoo.com. It is not the intent of the author to defame, harm or belittle any particular entity. Please stop reading if you develop signs of hopelessness, dizziness or lethargy. Ask your librarian if this publication is right for you. Please do not read this publication while driving, as doing so may cause an increased risk of crashing. No animals were harmed during any phase of writing, editing or publishing this book.

This book is intended as a guide, to educate, inform and entertain. Every effort has been made to make the document as accurate as possible. The author assumes no responsibility or liability for any errors, omissions or contrary interpretations of the subject matter herein. The reader is responsible for his or her own actions and the author does not assume any liability or responsibility whatsoever to any person or entity with regard to any loss or damage caused or alleged to be caused, directly or indirectly, by this document. Any trademarks, product names or services are assumed to be the property of their respective owners and are used only for reference. The book contains information only up to the date of the publication, including links to web pages, which may change in due course.

Editor: Faith Bicknell-Brown

Cover: Michael Tedesco Design

ISBN-13: 978-1495223495

ISBN-10: 1495223493

To Ann and Mike Tedesco,
for their eternal love and support.

One Man's Opinion

I like to see a man proud of the place in which he lives. I like to see a man live so that his place will be proud of him.

- Abraham Lincoln

Realizing that more wars and arguments are started over politics and religion, I've never been smart enough to learn from my mistakes. I'm confident that my comments and accusations encompassed within will piss off a great many people, but like other proud Americans, I'm fed up with our current dismal state of affairs. Analogous to many of my fellow countrymen, I'm deeply concerned with the ominous direction our country is headed and the incompetence of our corrupt and self-serving leaders guiding us down this dismal path. I'm concerned about the systematic and intentional downsizing of our middle class and the alarming number of people now living in poverty. It's becoming more apparent that the focus has shifted from an altruistic desire to help those in need to an insidious attempt by our federal government to seize total control and power. Poverty breeds poverty, and this growing dependence on entitlement programs, propagated and encouraged by the government, is jeopardizing our very future. More people in the United States currently live in poverty than any other time in our country's history. I love this great nation and I'm fed up with the negligence and venomous corruption spewing from Washington. The overwhelming amount of lies being told by our congressional delegates on a daily basis has grown to monumental proportions. I'm exhausted watching the majority of our citizens sit back and do nothing while our country, our civil rights and freedoms, granted under the constitution and our future, are slowly weaned from us. If we don't wake up soon and demand justice, all may be lost! Somewhere along the way our public officials forgot that they work for us. A vote is a powerful tool, so use it wisely and frequently. Sir Francis Bacon once said, *"Knowledge is power."* Arm yourselves before our collective voice ceases to matter.

Growing up in New York, I never had aspirations of running for political office nor expressed a keen devotion to any particular party. Raised republican, I was never particularly drawn to vote along party lines. Even though my parents are, and grandparents were, republicans, I was never pushed into committing to any political agenda, nor did my parents ever coerce their political views upon me or my siblings. I'll admit that over the last several years my allegiance has shifted to a more conservative fiscal approach. I don't feel that big government and surplus spending is the answer to solving the country's problems. You can't spend your way out of a debt crisis by continually printing more money. In the short-run, this plan works, because it keeps interest rates down, but in the long-run we will eventually dig ourselves a hole from which we can't climb out. We are now seventeen trillion in debt and this number grows by a trillion dollars every year. The Federal Reserve currently prints eighty-five billion dollars each month to help pay the interest on our growing debt. I was reading somewhere that we now pay roughly thirty cents on each dollar just to reimburse the interest on our loans. What will happen when our debt reaches twenty five trillion? This is not an unlikely scenario since the current administration seems complacent in continually growing our debt and offers no sound solutions for curbing their spending. In fact, Mr. Obama once again petitioned to raise the debt ceiling, getting us into further trouble. He blames the republicans for not compromising on this issue, but eventually our creditors are going to say "screw you", and then what do we do? And by the way, does anyone remember that for the first time in our nation's history our credit rating was downgraded, both times under this current administration? One might argue that it doesn't matter if global interest rates are high, but if the interest rates climb to a modest 6%, we will end up paying our creditors thirty-four trillion on our current debt over the next thirty years. This is an insurmountable figure. If we default on our loans or if there is a collapse of the US dollar, we could see hyperinflation in this country soar to levels unseen since The Great Depression. Commodity prices like food, bread and gasoline may cost many times what they do today, making the economic meltdown of 2008 look meek in comparison. The US dollar is our most precious and sacred commodity—it's what drives the world's economy. However, if we as a nation are unable to control our spending, our proprietary privileges may soon be a thing of the past.

China, Russia and France are currently meeting in secret to discuss ways to wean themselves off the American Dollar. If this happens, we as Americans are all screwed! Romney, in the 2012 Presidential Debate stated that if elected president he would declare China a currency manipulator. I may be naive when it comes to finance, but I don't blame China for attempting to distance themselves from the US currency. Would you want to go down with a sinking ship? If we don't start controlling our spending and pay down our debt, we will soon cease to exist as a great nation.

I did vote for democratic president, Bill Clinton twice, and to this day, I don't regret my decision. His moral ethics aside, I think he made a fine leader and our country prospered during his tenure as president. I firmly believe that it was Mr. Clinton's ability to reach across party lines and negotiate with Congress that led to his success in the White House. This was especially true of President Clinton and the Congress coming together to address and reform the entitlement programs hindering our country's growth. Today we have nearly fifty-million people collecting food stamps and another six million on disability—the largest number in our nation's history. Is it any wonder that we as a nation have experienced little or no economic growth within the last five years? What minute growth the country does generate is mostly from government buying and selling. This is no way to run a successful economy. I'm a fan of Bill Clinton, but I was gravely disappointed when he spoke at the Democratic Convention and told the American people that the republican's plans for recovering the economy doesn't add up. He said it was basic arithmetic that their strategy would fail. Well let me tell you, Mr. Clinton, I went to grade school and the most basic fundamental arithmetic calculation I can surmise is that we can't continue to spend as a nation more than we are earning!

I turned eighteen on the very day of the 1984 Presidential Election and as a birthday gift, I was afforded the opportunity to vote for the leader of the greatest country on Earth. In my eyes it was a privilege to participate in the electoral process and the selection of the ultimate leader whom would govern our nation for the subsequent four years. To me it was and still is the highest honor bestowed upon a citizen of this great country. Not only is it an honor, but I feel it's every American citizen's fiduciary responsibility to vote in an election for the person they feel would best represent the needs of the American people. It's the greatest entitlement we have as Americans. I voted for, Ronald Reagan, whom I still consider one of our finest presidents.

I guess things have changed a great deal since I was a young man. Perhaps the stiff reins of complacency and anarchy have strangled the very life out of the values that once made this country so great. We as a society have shifted focus. We no longer reward our entrepreneurial risk-takers and hard workers—we ostracize them. A sense of pride in one's accomplishments has taken a backseat to impetuousness and an overwhelming perception of entitlement that now plagues the youth of our nation. We shift blame instead of coming together to conquer our problems and differences. Successful people these days are frowned upon for their prosperity. There is this false notion that if you're successful in business, you didn't earn it, that somehow you finagled it from those less fortunate. Gee, I wonder from where this sentiment originated? Does anyone still remember that President Obama once said that if you achieved success, you didn't earn it, that you had help? Well, Mr. Obama, I'm the sole proprietor of a small, but successful brokerage firm. I'm not rich by any standard, but I'm proud to say that I had absolutely no government assistance in developing my business. To continue my success, I work almost every day and I can't remember the last time I went on a vacation. Meanwhile, Mr. President, you took almost one hundred-and-fifty golf outings (over 8% of your time in office) and went on numerous vacations at the taxpayer's expense in your first five years as president.

Presidential Candidate Mitt Romney was scorned for his wealth by the current administration during the past presidential election. The president and his cabinet claimed that Romney was a tax cheat because he paid taxes at 14%, which is the correct and legal statutory capital gains rate. And by the way, Mitt Romney gave away 30% ($2,000,000) of his income last year to charity. A donation percentage much greater than President Obama and Vice President Joe Biden combined.

With a current net worth of two-hundred and fifty million dollars, Mr. Romney would be a billionaire today if he stayed on course with the company he helped create: Bain Capital. All the other founders of the company are now billionaires, but Mr. Romney left the company to help serve the public sector. During the 2012 Presidential Election, Mr. Romney was harshly berated in the media for his success. I suppose it's wrong to be an accomplished business man, raising five drug-free, well-educated children, married to the same woman for the last thirty-eight years, the pastor of a church, the guy who turned Massachusetts's economy and education system around and saved the Olympics. I can see where the opposition would not hesitate to attack his character. I'm convinced that Americans lost a tremendous opportunity not having him as our leader. Besides, since when is it a sin to be wealthy in our country? There were many successful, wealthy presidents in our nation's history, many of whom were Democrats: LBJ, JFK, FDR, Clinton, Andrew Jackson, Jimmy Carter, etc. So to say that a rich president is an ineffectual leader is a statement geared at diverting attention away from the failed policies of the current administration. Wasn't it Barack Obama who said in 2008 *"If you don't have a policy to run on, then you make a big campaign about small issues?"* I would think birth control is a smaller issue than focusing attention on the dismal state of our floundering economy. Is Sandra Fluke still griping about this topic?

Our grandparents and great grandparents came to this country with nothing but the shirts on their backs and the shoes on their feet. They had very little in the way of earthly possessions, but were grateful for the hopes and dreams America offered—hopes and dreams that we, as a declining society, now take for granted. It seems we've fallen a great distance from the integrity of the constitution and the vision of our Founding Fathers. It wasn't that long ago that John F. Kennedy once said, *"Ask not what your country can do for you, but ask what you can do for your country."* It seems several generations later that narrative has been lost and our political leaders have waned from the mandates of our constitution—the law of our land. They've placed themselves above the rules that govern us, granting themselves special benefits and privileges not available to the average American. We've lost sight of what made us great in the first place. It wasn't overimposing government regulations that catapulted us to the pinnacle of the greatest super power the world had ever know; it was the many cultures coming together, putting aside their differences to think out of the box and work together to achieve great things. Nowadays our government has us so divided that blacks resent whites, old resent young, poor resent rich and, according to the president, the republicans are anti-woman and anti-gay (even though it's Obama who continues to flip-flop on his views regarding same-sex marriage depending on what is politically advantageous at that particular moment). Stated by our president and vice president, the republicans also intend on sending all illegal immigrants back to their respective countries without due process. I hear that the GOP is anti-senior citizen. During the 2012 election, Obama's committee to reelect ran an advertisement indicating that Mitt Romney and Paul Ryan intended to push a wheelchair-bound granny off the cliff, when in fact it was Obama who robbed Medicare, siphoning $716 billion from the program to help pay for Obamacare. Wasn't it Alexander the Great who once said that the best way to defeat your enemy is to divide and conquer? Besides the Civil War and the Civil Rights movement, I can't think of a more prominent time in American history where we as a nation are more polarized?

Not only are our people divided, but our leaders can't agree on any course of action to fix our impending doom. The inept house and the senate can't seem to see eye to eye on anything these days. If there is a conflict of interest amongst our congressional leaders, isn't it the responsibility of our president to reach across the aisle and get both parties negotiating on a solution to our problems? Isn't it a fundamental trait of a successful leader that he or she is also a master negotiator or, at the very least, doesn't create more disengagement between parties? That he or she is not only a compelling orator but a good listener? It's very tough to come to a compromise if one party is force-feeding its policies down the other party's throat without giving that silenced group the opportunity to provide input. Wasn't it Mr. Obama who once said, *"You can't change Washington from the inside?"* Obama, during his first year as president, provided a stimulus-bailout program to the tune of almost one trillion dollars (at the taxpayer's expense) to greedy, incompetent banks and automotive and insurance companies. In the eyes of our government, these industries were "Too big to fail!" There was no input from the republicans on the bill, because at the time, Obama controlled both the house and senate for his first two years in office. People seem to forget that Mr. Obama had total reins on spending and legislative power at this time and his policies still flopped, but yet he continues to divert blame to others and we the people and our liberal media fail to hold him accountable for his nonperformance. He claims it was either President Bush's fault or the fault of the republicans why things took a turn for the worse. What's baffling to me is that no one ever questioned President Obama after the stimulus package failed miserably. I'm no expert in fiscal policy, but if you're going to dole out that much *dinero*, shouldn't you draft legislation making sure that the stimulus money trickled down to small businesses and the middle class? The program failed, because the banks tightened up on lending. They sat on their assets and got fat while the rest of us witnessed our earning potential and the equity in our homes dwindle considerably. I understand the banks' reasoning. They were most likely gun-shy at the prospect of loaning money to people even if these people had sterling credit, because they didn't want to lose their shirts again. That's all well and good, but bailing out these large conglomerates didn't help the American people. I don't know about your neighborhood, but in my town it seems like the only new businesses cropping up nowadays are banks. Many believe that the repeal of the Glass-Steagall Act in 1999 was largely to blame for the housing market collapse back in 2008, which limited the exchange of security transactions from commercial banks to security firms. Once the law was nullified, the risk to lending institutions partaking in reckless ventures decreased. Since the Glass-Steagall repeal, the financial corporations are now essentially playing with the House's money. Contrary to Mr. Obama's pledge to make the rich pay their fair share financial institutions like Citicorp, Chase Manhattan, J.P. Morgan, and Wells Fargo have all doubled in size within the last decade.

If these institutions get involved with bad deals that go south and they lose money, their loss is now recompensed by the US government. If there's no risk for shady deals and poor decisions, then the frequency of these poor decisions will increase. It's like going to a Las Vegas casino and the casino tells me that I can gamble as much as I want. If I win, I keep my money, but is I lose, the casino will excuse my loss. I'll gamble more often, because I can't lose. The casino will in turn assume a larger portion of my growing debt. If the casino can only lose and I can only win, in the end I'll be rich and the house will go broke. Case in point, during the housing collapse, the banks loaned billions of dollars to first-time homeowners with either bad credit or no credit history. It's no wonder that a mass majority of these homeowners defaulted on their loans leading to record-high foreclosures and a depression in the housing market. What did the United States Government then do? They bailed the banks out to a tune of almost a trillion dollars. This was a trillion dollars of tax-payer's money. The American people got shafted and the banks got richer. Likewise, since the repeal of Glass-Steagall, it's easier for banks and security firms to collude. Contrary to the best interests of the public, banks now hold a majority role in the securities market.

I'm glad the American automotive industry reinvented themselves and are now on the path to success, but I wish the United States Government offered me a fifty-billion-dollar loan that I never had to repay. As a matter of fact, during the General Motors bailout, Obama illegally short-changed investors entitled for compensation, ignored the bankruptcy laws and reallocated the funds to top union executives. In a 2012 report furnished by the Mercatus Research Center dealing with the topic of political cronyism, the paper asserts that: "Of course, a much larger instance of cronyism under the Obama administration, one that makes the Solyndra case tiny by comparison, is the bailout of General Motors (GM) and

Chrysler. Bush and Obama together diverted $77 billion in TARP funds to GM and Chrysler. In organizing their bailouts and bankruptcies, Obama violated the rights of Chrysler's creditors and gave a sweetheart deal to the United Auto Workers union."[1] Chrysler Motors, investors were forced to accept twenty-nine cents on the dollars, while the Union Auto Workers received more than forty cents on the dollar.

Author David. R. Henderson for a leader dedicated to protecting the middle class and the poor in this country, the president didn't hesitate to bail out some of our wealthiest corporations—bailouts that aren't accessible to you or me. We now find that after the government sold off their remaining shares of GM, they took a net loss of $10 billion. Again this is a tremendous waste of taxpayer money!

I once worked as a medical malpractice claims analyst for the large insurance company on Wall Street that Obama bailed out. They shall remain nameless, but I have nothing good to say about them. During my time there, my

---

[1] David R. Henderson, "THE ECONOMICS AND HISTORY OF CRONYISM," Mercatus Center – George Mason University, July 27, 2012.

supervisors were ecstatic over the deaths of small children and infants that where covered under the policies of said insurance company, because they were no longer required by law to indemnify these claims. If the ailing baby lives and was maimed, the insurance company is required to pay out over the entire life of this infant, making the indemnification much more expensive in the long run. These heartless people eventually asked me to leave their company, because they said I was "too nice" for the job. To prove my point, the first thing these insurance executives did with the bail-out money was pay themselves multi-million-dollar bonuses at the taxpayer's expense.

Chapter 2

What makes us who we are?

I believe that there is definitive moment in time that defines each and every one of us as individuals. My mother once told me, "If you work hard and stay out of trouble, you'll get ahead." I've lived by this mantra most of my life. It wasn't always easy, but in the end I'm generally pleased with the results. I'm also an advocate of Sigmund Freud's *Pleasure Principal*,[2] which states that all humans, by instinct, seek pleasure and avoid pain in order to satisfy their biological and psychological needs. The economy certainly isn't getting better, so do we have to wait until things get so bad that we can't feed ourselves and our children before we will demand justice? Have we become so complacent in our societal roles that we're willing to give up our dreams and freedoms just to make ends meet?

The reason I decided to write this book is because of an incident I recently experienced at a local fast food restaurant. After school one day, my son asked me to take him to the fast-

---

[2] Snyder, C. R.; Lopez, Shane J. (2007). *Positive Psychology*. Sage Publications, Inc. p. 147. ISBN 0-7619-2633-X.

food restaurant. My wife was working that particular afternoon and, being the klutz in the kitchen that I am, I agreed to treat my son. While in line at the cash register, there was a lady in front of me. I eavesdropped on the conversation between the lady and the cashier taking her order. The customer was commending the young order-taker on his meritorious work ethic. He apparently worked a double shift that day and was exhausted from his efforts. As the manager of the store walked by, the customer asked the manager why the young man was mandated to work such long hours. The manager replied that the restaurant was having trouble hiring extra help. She addressed the customer's concerns, indicating that the young people that they usually employ have no motivation to work, that they are collecting more in the form of government aid then they would earn by actually working at the eatery. This revelation was a shocking epiphany for me. How are we going to survive as a nation in the long term if our government is promoting wide-spread laziness and complacency?

Wasn't it communist Russia that collapsed because their leaders promoted the same apathetic work ethic? They instructed their people that the government would take care of its citizens' basic necessities and give them everything they need to survive, but the people of Russia would never accomplish more out of life than what the government dictated. Eventually, the complacent Russian society, realizing that they'd never achieve anything enhancing their meek existence, stopped trying to better themselves. There was no reason to work hard, to innovate and challenge fundamental modes of thinking, to achieve success. Their government told them what to believe and how to act and eventually communist Russia fell. Does anyone else see the alarming similarities between us and communist Russia's failed policies?

I'm an advocate of our welfare system, but only if it is conducted without widespread abuse and corruption. The Department of Agriculture estimated in 2012 that welfare fraud reached $750 million. This figure spiked, more than doubling the 2006 to 2008 projection. Food stamps are being illegally resold on the open market to food retailers.[3] It's also a statistical conclusion that people receiving unemployment benefits don't aggressively start looking for work until their

---

[3] Huff Post Business, "Food Stamp Fraud Targeted As Election Season Brings Criticism," 02/06/2012 5:00 am.

benefits are scheduled to expire. Therefore, the federal government backing programs extending unemployment benefits from six months to almost ninety-nine months isn't helping the unemployed individual or the economy. Logically speaking, an employer is more apt to hire a job applicant displaced from the workforce for six months over an applicant that hasn't worked in nearly five years.

I understand that there are single mothers out there who need government assistance and those who are jobless are entitled to unemployment benefits, but the fact that nearly twenty percent of our country's population is out of work for an extended period is staggering. Under President Bush, thirty-two million people were collecting food stamps. Under the Clinton administration there were sixteen million. The staggering numbers today have grown to almost fifty million people. How can we expect to survive as a nation, if more people are taking from the system than contributing to it? So when Mr. Obama gets on the television and tells the American people that he wants the rich to do their fair share and contribute more, in reality he is telling the hard-working middle-class tax payers to pick up the extra burden, stretch their already limited budgets and pony-up more of their hard-earned dollars. Recently the federal government raised the payroll tax. Personally, as a sole proprietor, I'm paying $2,500 more in Social Security tax then I was a year ago. So when Obama tells us he is out to help the middle class and he is trying to lower their taxes, don't believe the hype. Under George W. Bush, average middle-class incomes rose 10% annually while under this current administration, average incomes declined 10%.

I got a kick out of watching Joe Biden's speeches during the last presidential election. He expressed to the American people that the current administration was a champion of the middle class. That our country's executive branch was responsible for regulating Wall Street. I found this statement humorous. Isn't Wall Street a symbol of America's wealth? I don't play the stock market, but didn't The DOW Jones, Nasdaq and S&P 500 soar to record highs in recent years while the rest of us saw our savings and pensions dwindle? Under Obamacare, the president not only exempted himself and Congress from participating in the new health care policy, but he granted waivers to 1,400 large businesses and unions, deferring the employer mandate for a year. Does anyone else feel that it's unfair and unlawful for the president to pick and choose those absolved from participating in the new law while the rest of us working slobs get shafted? So isn't it accurate to say that the rich keep getting richer under this president while the poor and the shrinking middle class suffer the most? How did Mr. Biden claim to regulate Wall Street when gas and commodities prices are double from when Mr. Obama first took office?

I didn't vote for Obama in 2008 because of his pledge to raise taxes on those making over a certain income. I'm not a wealthy man, but I comprehended this to mean that he intended to raise taxes on all. While campaigning in the 2008 election, then candidate Barak Obama promised: *"I can make a firm pledge: Under my plan, no family making less than $250,000 a year will see any form of tax increase. Not your income tax, not your payroll tax, not your capital gains taxes, not any of your taxes."*[4] Once he was elected to office, we now see that this was a fallacious promise broken many times. During a primary debate in 2008 against then opponent, Hilary Clinton, Obama pledged never to strong-arm anyone to buy health insurance, but in 2010 he shoved Obamacare down our throats.

---

[4] Guy Benson, "Flashback Videos: Obama's False Tax Promises," Townhall.com, Jun 28, 2012.

Even though I didn't vote for Obama in 2008, I was excited when he pledged to wean us off our dependency on foreign oil, that he was committed to drilling in our country and also investigating other avenues of alternative energy. We now learn that this was just another broken campaign promise. Now that we are paying nearly twice as much at the pump as we did when Obama first took office, we are no closer to achieving energy independency. We currently buy $75 billion of crude oil from OPEC each year. Even if we decrease our dependency on foreign oil, what good does it do the American people? If we increase our fracking efforts in this country or create the Alaskan Pipeline, we will continue to be held hostage by the greedy oil conglomerates, special interest groups and the United States Government. There is no incentive for our government to wean us off oil. They make more in the form of taxes from oil sales than anyone. Why should they change this? Joe Biden said he helped regulate Wall Street, but do you realize Wall Street controls 80% of the oil future markets. We as Americans pay on average forty cents more a gallon on gasoline than we should due to greedy oil speculators. Just ten years ago speculators controlled only 30% of the market. So as long as there is unethical stock manipulation, the American public will not see relief at the pump.

Further hindering our aspirations for energy independence, Obama single-handedly dismantled our coal industry by enacting unrealistic and unattainable EPA regulations geared at controlling carbon dioxide emissions. A study by the Heritage Foundation found that the new regulations would essentially eliminate a half million jobs in the coal industry over the next fifteen years, which would inadvertently increase electric costs by upwards of 20%. I recently received a notice from the electric company that my rates were increasing by 20%. A 2009 article published by the Science and Public Policy Institute estimates that the total impact by The United States stopping all carbon dioxide emissions in this country would result in a miniscule decrease of .08% Celsius in global warming in the next forty years.

Speaking of raising gas taxes, I'm from Connecticut. We just had our gas prices recently increased to almost twenty-three cents a gallon in one week. How anyone can vote for Democrat, Dannel Malloy in the next election is beyond my reasoning. Here is a guy that came in and raised taxes to balance the state budget to the tune of many billions of dollars in his first two years as governor. He raised the gas tax twice, the sales tax, state income tax, estate tax and created a whole bunch of fun new taxes. He did this in a time when our middle class is mightily struggling. Under Governor Malloy's leadership, Connecticut has seen the largest tax hikes in our state's history, but we citizens of the state have experienced little relief or benefit from the extra burden. After all his efforts, the state is no better off financially than when he took office. He should be ashamed of himself, and I hope the good people of Connecticut have the common sense to not reelect him in next year's election. Wasn't Malloy a huge proponent of Obamacare and couldn't wait to jam it down the throats of Connecticut residents?

Chapter 3

Does redistribution of wealth work?

Many countries tried over the last
century to redistribute wealth to its people and
only succeeded in redistributing poverty. The
main reason why redistribution doesn't work is
because the heads of state can only seize wealth
at that present moment. They cannot seize
future wealth because it doesn't exist. A time-
worn adage comes to mind when I think of the
Robin Hood concept of taking from the rich
and giving to the poor. It's an old Chinese
proverb, which says: *"Give a man a fish and
you feed him for a day. Teach a man to fish and
you feed him for a lifetime."* I was reading
somewhere that if our federal government
seized all of the assets of those wealthy
Americans making over a million dollars a
year, the increased revenue wouldn't come
close to solving our fiscal crisis. "It's a fantasy
to imagine that raising taxes on the rich will
solve our deficit problem. If the IRS grabbed
100 percent of income over $1 million, the take
would be just $616 billion. That's only a third
of this year's deficit. Our national debt would

continue to explode."[5] So, taking from the rich will not put a dent in our problems. Also, the rich are not stupid, most of them are experts on managing their wealth and will find loopholes in the system and ways to hold onto their assets. "Higher taxes give rich people and politicians more reasons to collude. The rich make contributions to political campaigns, and politicians pay the rich back by giving them tax loopholes."[6]

The liberal media contend that the current administration's plot to redistribute wealth in the country is unfounded, but the statistics don't lie. A new study by the Congressional Budget Office found that the top 40% of earners in United States pay 106% of the nation's income taxes, while the bottom 40% contribute -9%. The bottom 40% of the nation, per capita, drain the system on average $19,000 annually.[7] Under the Obamacare

---

[5] Dan Bigman (Managing Editor for Business News), "John Stossel: Tax The Rich? The Rich Don't Have Enough. Really," Forbes, 4/03/2012 @ 2:39PM.

[6] Dan Bigman, Forbes, 4/03/2012 @2:39PM.

[7] Terence P Jeffrey, CBO:Top 40% Paid 106.2% of Income Taxes; Bottom 40% Paid -9.1%, Got Average of Jeffrey, Terence P. December 9, 2013 - 2:21 PM.

provisions roughly 50% of the country will receive FREE healthcare benefits, while the other 50% will incur the costs of these benefits. The 50% footing the entire bill will become indebted with high premiums and high deductibles to pay for everyone's medical costs, while the 50% receiving this free healthcare will pay little or no out-of-pocket medical expenses. Universal healthcare is nothing more than a blatant tool used to redistribute wealth.

Redistributing wealth is an even more ineffectual policy in today's world, because we now live in an industrial technologically-rich environment. Years ago when the government attempted to seize wealth, they focused their efforts primarily on seizing property from farmers and wealthy land owners, but in today's society, the rich are not tied to their land. They can distribute personal wealth to foreign countries, building up the economies of these countries instead of our own. Large American businesses manufacturing abroad to

---

CBO:Top 40% Paid 106.2% of Income Taxes; Bottom 40% Paid -9.1%, Got Average of $18,950 in 'Transfers'. CNSNews.com. http://cnsnews.com/news/article/terence-p-jeffrey/cbotop-40-paid-1062-income-taxes-bottom-40-paid-91-got-average-18950#sthash.cPId7stQ.dpuf.

keep overhead down is a prime example of this in today's commerce. Donald Trump recently commented that *"The wealthy today are international... they're not tied to any particular country."*

Another problem with redistributing wealth is that once people see the government seizing their assets, then the ambition to create future wealth becomes hindered. People are not willing to work hard and risk it all only to see their belongings taken from them. You have to ask yourself why a smart Harvard man like Barack Obama, who knows that redistribution of wealth is a futile approach to running an economy just by examining the histories of those countries who tried it and failed, would push his socialist agenda and try to redefine America. It was our fundamental capitalistic ideologies, which made our country great in the first place. Why reinvent the wheel? Our democracy wrote the book on the formula for success, so why not learn from our own past. The point being that redistributing wealth has never worked at any time in any country!

Not only are we redistributing wealth within America nowadays, but we are also redistributing our wealth to other countries. Right now, we as a nation cannot compete on a global market. Our small businesses and corporations pay the second highest corporate taxes in the world, and since Japan is in the process of lowering their corporate tax rate, we will soon be the highest. We can no longer compete on the international level, because it is cheaper for many of our companies to produce goods and services overseas. Our current administration provides very little incentives and tax breaks to those manufacturers producing goods and services in this country. It's not rocket science why our blue-collar labor force is quickly losing ground to cheaper labor sources throughout the world. There has been a rapid decline in American manufacturing over the years. We have shifted from an industrial based to a financial based economy. As a matter of fact, Mr. Obama created only three international trade agreements during his first term as president (all started under the Bush administration). Meanwhile, China created seventeen trade agreements in that same time period. Forbes Magazine recently inferred in an article that by the time Mr. Obama leaves office we could no longer be the world leading economy. "It isn't certain that China will become No 1 by the time President Obama leaves office, as argued in a previous piece here. But it is destined to happen in the near future, given the country's huge population and labor force and export industrialization drive—provided that No 1 means the country with the world's largest GDP."[8] China has already surpassed us in many industries, including the production of automobiles, steel and electronics. They are also now the world's leader in foreign aid to struggling nations.

Class warfare and the redistribution of wealth doesn't breed success it breeds destitution. Just ask the people of Cuba. When Cuban revolutionary, Fidel Castro seized power in the 1950's after a violent revolution he implemented socialist reforms. His failed Marxist-Leninist approach to governing set his country back to the stone-age, imprisoning his people in a perpetual state of pauperism and sending Cuba floundering to the solemn depths of an impoverished third-world country.

Right now one in six people in this country lives in poverty. This is the highest

---

[8] Panos Mourdoukoutas, Contributor, "What It Takes For China To Be No 1," Forbes, 4/01/2013 @ 7:56PM.

number in our nation's history. Mr. Obama has spent his entire time in office pledging allegiance to our country's poor, but under his watch our poverty has grown out of control. According to the last election, fifty-two percent of the nation continue to support the president on his efforts. I don't understand how we as a nation can reelect a leader who has failed by his own admission and hasn't lived up to his own standards. Back in 2008, while still a presidential candidate, Mr. Obama stated that if he couldn't curtail our employment rate below 5.5%, if he couldn't wean us off foreign oil, and if he couldn't reduce our debt to a manageable level, then he would be a one-term president. Well, five years later, we are seven trillion dollars deeper in debt, our unemployment rate hovers over 8% for more than half a decade and we are no closer to energy independence then we were before he first took office. In today's workforce nearly twenty-three million people are unemployed or underemployed. This is an alarming and unacceptable figure. If I as a small business owner ran my company this ineptly, I'd be out of business within six months, yet as citizens of this great country we praise our congressional leaders for running the largest business on earth into the ground. We reward them with extended terms and special privileges when the only thing they seem to agree upon today is to raise their own salaries.

Not only are we redistributing our wealth from the more affluent to the indignant masses, but we are also transferring wealth internationally. Besides the fact that our high corporate tax rate is encouraging US companies to conduct business abroad, our federal government is promoting programs to distribute wealth to other countries. Fisker, an automotive manufacturer from Finland, was awarded a $530 million contract to build hybrid electric cars, despite the fact that the cars cost well over a $100,000 to build and they are faulty. The bankrupt company suspended automobile production in November 2012 siting "financial difficulties."[9] This was a huge waste of taxpayer's money. Obama expressed a desire to elevate the price of gasoline in a devious plot to make green companies appear more affordable. He imposed a moratorium, restricting oil drilling in this country and shut down construction of the Keystone Pipeline. Blocking the pipeline prevented synthetic oil from funneling to the states from Alberta Canada, forcing the Canadian's to sell their oil

[9] Bradley Berman (2013-03-13), "Henrik Fisker Resigns From Fisker Automotive." *The New York Times*, Retrieved 2013-06-18.

to China.[10] He blocked the Alaskan pipeline, hindering our ability to become more energy self-sufficient and then invested two billion dollars into the Brazilian government's efforts to drill oil in their country. To add salt to the wound, Obama then pledged to Brazil that the US would become one of their largest consumers, further hindering our dreams of energy independence.[11] Last but not least, Obama sunk billions into bankrupt "green" companies like, Solyndra, SpectraWatt, First Solar and the Willard & Kelsey Solar Group. In fact, the federal government subsidized thirty-four such alternative energy companies that are either faltering or have filed for bankruptcy. This is an obscene waste of taxpayer money and to date not one person was ever held accountable for this grave miscalculation.

Solyndra is a prime example of the corruption spewing from Washington these days. After Pricewaterhouse Coopers LLP, a

---

[10] John MacHaffie, "The Complete List of Barack Obama's Scandals, Misdeeds, Crimes and Blunders," REPUBLIC NOW - Galactic News, September 17th, 2013.

[11] John MacHaffie, REPUBLIC NOW - Galactic News, September 17th, 2013.

consulting and tax firm, audited Solyndra and designated the company financially unsound, President Obama, against the advice of the auditors, granted the floundering company a $530 million federal loan. Two days after Solyndra's public offering, in an effort to raise capital to keep the company solvent, the company conspicuously filed for bankruptcy. The unethical undertaking left investors high and dry. Subsequently, the FBI was called in to investigate the matter. They raided the building and seized company records, but no indictments were issued to date and the money trail dubiously disappeared.[12]

By his own words, Mr. Obama has failed us as a leader, but we don't recognize his admission because Mr. Obama is an expert in using the liberal media to pass blame, especially when it comes to his failed policies. He blames President Bush for creating the country's mess in the first place. Even when he had total control of both the house and senate during his first two years as president and was able to pass everything on his political agenda. Back in 2008, Obama declared then President

---

[12] Jim Snyder & Christopher Martin – "Obama Team Backed $535 Million Solyndra Aid as Auditor Warned on Finances," *Bloomberg News, Sep 12, 2011 12:59 PM ET.*

Bush *"Unpatriotic"*, because the president raised the national deficit to a half trillion dollars a year. However, under the fiscally irresponsible Obama Administration, the deficit has increased three times this rate. Many Americans are still waiting for Obama to apologize for his contradictory remarks, but don't hold your breath. The stimulus package was a colossal failure. Obamacare is proving to be a huge detriment to our country and will most likely bankrupt us.

Mr. Obama blamed President Bush during the last presidential debates for the prodigious decline in our nation's economy. Obama further implied that his policies stopped the bleeding and we have to stay the course in order to reap the benefits of his grand scheme. During the Democratic Convention he said, *"We can't quit now, we have to finish what we started."* Five years later does anyone still believe the president's policies are helping? I really don't think that President Bush was an effective leader, but he is a moral man who loves this country. He got us involved in an unpopular war and drove our debt up four trillion dollars in his eight years in office, but at least he was smart enough to allow the American economy to run itself. He didn't raise taxes on the middle class and impose harsh restrictions and regulations on small businesses. His tax refunds and lack of involvement in the economy actually helped the middle class see an increase in annual incomes to the tune of 10%.

We eventually ousted Saddam Hussein from power. Many people argued it was mistake going into Iraq and removing the Iraqi dictator and that no weapons of mass destruction were uncovered to demonstrate just cause. I'd argue that Hussein not only possessed weapons of mass destruction, but he used them. In 1988, the Bathe Regime headed by Hussein, launched thirty-nine separate toxic gas attacks on the rebel Kurds. He used the poisonous gas, Sarin to slaughter five thousand innocent men, women and children, but no mention of this was made extensively in the news. The Iraqi's coined Saddam the nickname, Chemical Ali for his use of unconventional warfare. The recent US–Russian agreement to dismantle chemical arms in Syria bears a striking resemblance to the chemical attacks in Iraq during the late 1980s, but many members of the press during the 2003 Iraq War failed to associate Saddam's use of chemical warfare as a weapon of mass destruction outlined under the Geneva Convention of 1949. They called the American attack on Iraq "unjustifiable" and our reasoning "unsubstantiated." Whether you agree or disagree with the war in Iraq, Saddam Hussein was a monster, responsible for the genocide of two million people. His dethroning from power was a necessity and his execution was "sweet justice."

While it's true that President Bush raised our debt by four trillion dollars, President Obama raised our debt by almost twice that in half the time. The current president blames his predecessor for our troubles, but let's take a look at where the money trail really leads. Obama spent a trillion dollars his first year in office to fund a failed stimulus program. He grew the size of the federal government a staggering 42% his first term in office. It costs us nearly a trillion dollars each year to run the federal government. He grew welfare, disability, unemployment and social security to outrageous numbers. Our entitlement programs now cost our country nearly a trillion dollars each year. He sunk billions into corrupt alternative energy programs that conspicuously went belly-up. Years later, we still don't know where this money trail leads. So when Mr. Obama says the outrageous debt compiled in Washington over the last several years is the result of Bush's failed policies, just remember that we won't experience real recovery in this nation until we address debt reduction and entitlement reform.

These are areas Mr. Obama won't even touch. In fact, this year Obama issued a directive, undermining the Welfare Reform Act passed by Congress during the Clinton Administration. Obama told the states that: "They are no longer obligated to comply with the welfare-to-work requirements, illegally dismissing the mandates of the law."[13] Why is this president intentionally trying to get the American people hooked on welfare and food stamps? Perhaps he feels that you can't buy votes if you're not giving away "freebies?"

Obama blames the republicans for the stalemate in Congress today. I can't recall a time in the last five years when President Obama actually reached across party lines in a bipartisan manner and negotiated with the other party, yet he criticizes the republicans for being rigid and unwavering. He reiterated to the American people that the recent shutdown of the federal government was a ploy by republicans to undermine his authority and attack his policies—that their attempt to defund Obamacare is hurting the economy. In fact, the republicans ventured to negotiate fourteen times with Harry Reid and President Obama to come to an understanding. Obama reiterated

---

[13] John MacHaffie, REPUBLIC NOW - Galactic News, September 17th, 2013.

that he would not make any concessions on his healthcare bill, period! How is it the republican's fault if they are trying to protect the interests of the American people and depose an unpopular health care bill that will eventually bankrupt the states and restrict hiring? If healthcare isn't a political power-play then why did President Obama tell the G.O.P. back in 2013 that he would veto any bill submitted by the house attempting to delay Obamacare for a year until the kinks were worked out. However, he then later turned around and delayed it a year unilaterally by his own authority? If it was the same idea, why not collaborate with the republicans to work out a bipartisan solution to an important topic that effects a sixth of our entire economy.

Fourteen times the republican leaders attempted to negotiate on Obamacare. They went from totally defunding the Affordable Health Act and repealing the bill to primarily demanding that everyone played by the same rules. Right now congress exempted themselves from participation in the program. If they do participate, they are given a 72% subsidy to pay for their healthcare. Likewise, fourteen-hundred companies were provided waivers deferring participation for a year. As a middle-class citizen of this country, I find it appalling that our legislative body imposing these unconstitutional mandates on the American people, has the audacity to exempt themselves from the very program that they praise. How dare they put themselves above the people they were sworn to serve and how dare Mr. Obama illegally select and choose those mandated from participating in the new law. Thank God for the conservative attempt to seek justice and equality for all. If the new law of the land is so great, then why are they exempting themselves from participating?

Chapter 4

What is the price of poverty?

This year alone the United States distributed nearly sixty billion dollars in foreign aid to roughly 180 countries. This amount is 1.5% of the entire federal budget. We gave $1.3 billion last year in aid to Pakistan after they knowingly concealed the world's most notorious terrorist from us. We gave $1.5 billion in aid to Mohamad Morsi and the Egyptian regime after they condoned the attack on our embassy in Cairo and then reprimanded us on our ethics. Morsi is the leader of the Muslim Brotherhood, a religious and socialist movement geared toward violence, and responsible for the ordination of the terrorist group, Hamas. We even gave twenty-eight million in foreign aid to the country that basically now owns us, China. Why are we giving so much help to foreign countries when we are flat broke? Why are we giving money to countries that we are borrowing money from and paying interest to? Wouldn't the funds best help those at home?

Right now fifty million people in this country live below the poverty level. Currently the unemployment rate hovers around 8%. The true unemployment rate is really around 14%.

Unemployment statistics only tally and incorporate the number of people collecting unemployment benefits. The figure doesn't include all the people who dropped out of the job market.

I understand there is a sense of pride amongst the African American community that we have our first black president, but you can't always judge a book by its cover and you can't always determine the quality of a leader by the color of his skin. The unemployment rate is 8% in this country, but the unemployment rate for the African American community is much higher, over 14% (this figure doesn't include all of the people no longer actively looking for work). If this wasn't bad enough, the unemployment rate for Latinos is even greater. Even though one in six Americans today live in poverty, the figures are substantially higher for blacks and Hispanics.

During the 2012 national conventions and presidential debates, I heard a lot coming from the liberals that Mr. Romney and the republicans are gender-bias and anti-women, because the conservatives were fundamentally pro-choice and deemed it unethical to pay for a women contraceptives. If anyone is anti-women, I'd argue that it's the current administration. Under President Obama's first term in office, women suffered the highest unemployment plaguing them in the last thirty years. As a member of the opposite sex, I realize I can't relate to the woes of the opposite gender, but I'd think feeding one's family would take precedence over fulfilling the gratification of one's sex life?

In the last election, a great majority of college students voted for the democratic presidential candidate, yet 50% of all college students can't find a meaningful job today after graduation. Why would anyone vote for a leader who is making it harder for them to obtain employment?

Wikipedia defines Welfare as "a provision of a **MINIMAL** level of **WELL-BEING** and social support for all its citizens." It is a system incorporated to help those in need, but in today's society, there are too many currently abusing the program. The problem with poverty is that it's a vicious cycle. Once you are condemned to the affliction of poverty, it's hard to free oneself from its barbarous grips. In the short term, a person collecting government assistance will attain interim satisfaction, but in the long-run the sacrifice of not having a skill set will greatly hinder this person's ability to function without the help of the government. So, when Joe Biden tells you that the republicans are keeping you in chains, then just look at the long-term detrimental effects his administration has done for those in need. Using the state of Ohio as an example, a family of four is only eligible to receive $506 a month in cash to pay bills. However, if you add food stamps to this, then for a family of four, in Ohio (each state and each county in each state are often different), will receive *approximately* $650 to $700 a month in stamps—only if there is absolutely <u>no income</u> of any sort coming into the home. The point being, don't sell your souls for several hundred dollars a week in government aid! You are a much more precious commodity than you think.

Also, the mortality rate for the impoverished is much greater than those more prosperous. Individuals with money can generally afford some or better healthcare. Under the Affordable Healthcare Act not everyone will have coverage and those who are covered will most likely see their insurance premiums skyrocket. It's estimated that thirty million Americans will remain without health benefits making Obamacare a moot point. With all the hospital and doctor office layoffs caused by the new health bill, it is only a matter of time before we see the quality of our healthcare in this country rapidly decline. A new survey conducted by trusted research firm, Deloitte

Center for Health Solution, found that six in ten doctors polled agree that a large percentage of senior physicians in this country will retire within the next three years due to the Obamacare mandates. A recent Nightly News segment on NBC recently charged that 75% of Americans who buy private healthcare will lose their benefits, because these plans don't live up to Obamacare standards (http://www.nbcnews.com/id/3032619/#53399 256). This is a far cry from the administration's prior assurances that Americans privately insured can keep their current plan. As a matter of fact, concealed within the 2010 Obamacare register report, a paragraph outlines a grisly prediction that the administration expects 40% to 67% of those privately insured will lose their current plan under the AHC Act.[14]

The most disheartening aspect of poverty is that those impoverished will most likely never achieve their life dreams and ambitions; they will never attain greatness and capture that sense of self-pride that is felt by the accomplishments of one's work. What's

---

[14] Igor Volsky, "Here Is What's Wrong With That Story About Obama Knowing That Your Health Care Policy Would Get Cancelled," ThinkProgress.org., October 28, 2013 at 8:59 pm.

worse is that the poor generally end up passing this poverty onto their children. This is perhaps the greatest tragedy of all. Subsequently, what happens when the system goes bankrupt and there is no more funding for government support? There's no doubt we are now headed down this path. I ask that if you neglect to contemplate your own future, just think of the future you are bequeathing to your children.

"The problems we face today are there because the people who work for a living are outnumbered by those who vote for a living."

–Rabbi Steven Pruzansky

Chapter 5

Are we headed for socialism?

Back in 2008, then presidential candidate, Barak Obama told Joe the Plumber that it's advantageous to spread the wealth around. In fact, back in the 90s Obama was governing members of a Chicago-based left-wing socialist group called the "New Party." The president has since tried to disassociate himself and sever ties with the radical left-wing organization, but it's a fact that while running for the Illinois state senate back in 1996, Obama signed the New Party Candidate Contract and sought the group's endorsement.[15]

Our Founding Fathers created a government predicated on a system of checks and balances. This is why our government is

---

[15] Stanley Kurtz, "Obama's Third Party History," The National Review Online, June 7, 2012 4:00 AM.

made up of three branches. They also drafted a constitution and a Bill of Rights to protect the rights and freedoms of average citizens, which specifically outlines the limits of government interference in our lives. The reason why Washington, Jefferson, Franklin and others adopted our democracy was so that different branches of the government can offset the influence of the others, thus insuring that one branch doesn't become too powerful. Following our nation's independence, we liberated ourselves from the tyrannical oppression of King George and the British Empire. We weren't about to devise a governing body capable of dictating our lives. We opposed one king and didn't want to substitute for another. In the olden days, British monarchs unilaterally suspended laws that didn't coincide with their governing agenda. Does this sound eerily familiar to what's going on in our government today?

Prior to the presidential election of 2012, during an interview on *60 Minutes*, President Obama explained to the commentator that if the Republicans didn't work with him on Healthcare and bend to his philosophy, then he would get his policies passed without their support. He further commented that his programs are good for the American people. I essentially read this statement to mean that we no longer have our system of checks and balances and that this president has instituted himself a dictator. How arrogant can one man be that he deems his intelligence superior to everyone else's? What if he's wrong and his policies are bad for our country? So far I'm not impressed with our lame recovery. Like so many, I feel this president is taking us down an irreversible path of inevitable destruction. Our debt in the end WILL kill us. There's never been a country in the history of the world that effectively bought themselves out of debt by continually spending. The United States is NO exception.

There seems to be little urgency nowadays for our president to reduce our debt. Quite the contrary, he wants Congress to raise the debt ceiling once again so he can borrow more money. He seeks unlimited spending power for his next three years as president. We see today that Obama is force-feeding his agenda down our throats without our support. When the republican Congressional leaders attempt to draw a redline opposing more government spending without endorsing programs geared towards cutting our inflated expenditures, they were ostracized in the liberal media and designated the "bad guys." In fact, we need sound people to stand up and oppose such harmful policies. We cannot continue spending more than we are earning. Our currency has devalued to where interest rates continue to hover at a historic all-time low. It's only a matter of time before we experience hyperinflation to the point where we will eventually find ourselves paying much more for commodities like food and gasoline.

I don't know about you, but I worship one messiah and it isn't our president. Since when in America does the will of 300 million bend to the whim of one man? Obamacare is utterly disregarding the laws of the constitution and infringing upon our freedom of choice. If you are in favor of Obamacare and you are one of the few that hasn't seen their premiums sky-rocket recently, then just remember that if you're willing to give up one freedom, you're willing to give them all up. Under this president, many of us experienced more stress, while watching the quality of our lives greatly diminish. We've been overtaxed, overworked, overregulated and overmanaged by an overimposing government. Imagine living in a country where the government regulates and mandates all of the choices of the lives of its citizens, where the government tells you what to think, how to act and what you can achieve in life. Under the Marxist model of socialism, the first step in heading down the path towards a socialist progressive state is a government takeover of the country's healthcare system. Sound familiar?

Is Obamacare really about the concerns of the nation's uninsured or is more about the government attempting to seize more power and control over your lives? They give you what they deem as affordable healthcare and you in return give them your vote in the next election. To prove my point…currently when you sign up for healthcare through the Obamacare exchange, voter registration forms are included with the application. What the hell does voting have to do with healthcare? Once the applicant completes the voter request forms, the government can now share this information with an unlimited host of liberal organization to persuade voting habits. The exchange is expected to enroll sixty-eight million new participants within the next three years. A good deal of these new inductees are low-income Americans. These applicants will receive free or extremely affordable healthcare. In return, these applicants will continue voting for the party responsible for giving them this free healthcare. It's voter fraud 101. The federal government is essentially saying, "If you scratch my back, I'll scratch yours."

In a recent Breitbart article entitled, "Election Integrity Activists: Obamacare 'Biggest Voter Registration Fraud Scheme in History,' "Several election integrity activists have alleged that the Patient Protection and Affordable Care Act (PPACA) or, Obamacare, does not appear to have been an effort to conduct healthcare reform to fix what was described in 2009 and 2010 as a broken healthcare system. The law passed Congress with just Democratic Party support. Instead of being an honest attempt to fix America's healthcare woes, I think [it] is the biggest voter registration fraud scheme in the history of the world," said Gregg Phillips, the founder of the election integrity group Voters Trust, in an interview with Breitbart News Wednesday morning." The article went on to further add that: "Engelbrecht and Phillips believe that all of those promises about healthcare were never meant to be true. They believe one of the underlying intents is to collect personal data and voter registration information and share it with the federal government, which would in turn share it with left-wing groups—in Obamacare they are called "Navigators"—to conduct what is essentially a taxpayer-funded Get-Out-The-Vote operation for the Democratic Party."[16]

Obama grew our federal government over 42% in his first four years in office, do you think these people are going to vote themselves out of office? 35% of the entire US labor force is currently comprised of government employees. Do you think these employees and elected officials aren't going to decree their respective offices special privileges and cave into the demands of special interest groups? We are already seeing it happen in Congress. They exempted themselves from Obamacare. As a member of Congress, if you serve only one term in office, you reap the benefit of a lifetime pension. The system is broken if our elected officials can fail miserably and still benefit from perks not offered to the majority of us.

I hear today in the liberal media that the republicans have hit an all-time low with regards to their approval rating. Feeling the pressure, the republicans recently caved in and reversed their decision to shut down the federal government. They realized that their actions

---

[16] Matthew Boyle, 'Election Integrity Activists: Obamacare 'Biggest Voter Registration Fraud Scheme in History,' Breitbart, 30 Oct 2013.

were hurting a good number of American citizens and that their struggle to defund a harmful presidential policy would not end well for many. Obama is effective in narrating to the American people that the republicans are solely responsible for the shutdown and that they jeopardized the recovery of the economy by their self-serving actions. He is an expert at pitting himself and everyone whom supports him against the rest of us. It's their fault things didn't turn out right! In the last five years has Obama ever professed to anything he's done wrong? Did he ever confess or atone to the massive number of people he's hurt? He recently apologized to the five million individuals kicked off their existing health care coverage due to Obamacare, but this insincere atonement came after massive pressure by his Democratic constituents to save the careers of the party members and appease the base. We now see that the democrats, who overwhelmingly supported Obamacare and pushed through the bill, are scattering. They're attempting to distance themselves from the president and his signature piece of legislation after they rammed this unpopular "law-of-the-land" down the throats of the American people. Why should we let these congressional leaders off the hook after they ignored the wishes of a large majority of the nation who didn't want the law passed to begin with? These politicians swore to fight for our interests and contrarily facilitated their own interests. We don't need self-serving people like this leading our country.

Initially, Obama blamed the insurance companies for failing to keep his promise that you can keep their current policy and current physicians. He still hasn't apologized to the nation for misleading us when he had prior knowledge that many would lose their existing coverage once the Obamacare mandates were launched. I'm a baseball fan and I cannot recollect an instance when a baseball manager blamed his players for their poor performance. No, the manager bears the brunt of the burden and takes responsibility as his role as the leader of the team. Yet, in politics, shifting blame seems to be the president's modus operandi. When are we going to have a leader with the integrity to take responsibility for the failed policies he implemented? You can't fix a problem if you don't admit there is a problem in the first place and "you can't have your cake and eat it too." If the president wants to make all of the decisions then why shouldn't he also then assume all of the consequences of these decisions? Describing the office of the presidency, Harry S. Truman once said, *"The buck stops here!"*

During Mr. Obama's first four years as president he had the luxury of passing most of his agenda without the support of a bipartisan Congress. He passed a very expensive stimulus bill and levied increased taxes against the top earners of our country. He passed sequestration, Cap & Trade and Obamacare. If the policies are failing and if negotiations over the years broke down on Capitol Hill, I argue that you can't blame the other side when you won't make concessions or negotiate with them. Why should Obama make concessions since he's gotten everything he wants anyway! I'm tired of hearing Obama's excuse that you can't change Washington from the inside. Many presidents were able to effectively reach across the table in a bipartisan manner and work with the opposition to draft ground-breaking legislation. President Clinton did this with entitlement reform, President Reagan was effective in adopting extensive immigration reform and President Kennedy was instrumental in enacting comprehensive civil rights legislation. Mr. Obama is the president of this nation so he should take responsibility and lead.

I agree that the republicans are demonstrating weak leadership. The divided party appears incapable of defending themselves against the bullying of the executive branch. However, without this system of checks and balances, there is very little preventing one party from dominating the American people. So far this president has shown very little respect for those who oppose his radical agenda. What happens if the republicans lose the house in 2014? If this should transpire then we are essentially living in a fascist state—many would argue that our democracy is a thing of the past. In a true democracy, the people elect policies and govern themselves. We technically live in a republic. The difference being that in a republic the populace elects officials who govern them and these elected officials spawn policy and laws to supervise the whole. If the American people deem the Republican Party's actions to shut down our government in order to defund Obamacare as wrongful, then please remember that during Obama's first two years as president, he passed a very expensive stimulus package without support or input of the republican delegates. To the chagrin of the republicans, he also passed a risky healthcare reform act. I think it's basic common sense that a rational person wouldn't support a radical bill like universal healthcare if they weren't privileged to read and review the documents that they were signing into law. The fundamental difference between Romneycare and Obamacare is that the republicans were told by then House Majority Leader, Nancy Pelosi, that if they wanted to see what was in the Affordable Healthcare Bill, they'd have to sign it first. So essentially the law was passed by one party, behind closed doors, without the support of the American people. More and more we now find ourselves condemned to overgovernment regulations. I can't remember a time in my life that I've been more stressed out and upset every time our government throws in their two cents. Representative Paul Ryan said in a 2012 House Budget Committee speech that, *"We're looking for bipartisan solutions, not partisan rhetoric. Exploiting people's emotions of fear, envy and anxiety is not hope, it's not change—it's partisanship."*

Many would argue that Obamacare is actually designed to destroy the private sector and create dependency on government assistance programs. The only thing stopping Obama from realizing his dreams of a socialized America is the republican's control of the House of Representatives. If the democrats gain control of the house in the 2014 election, there will be nothing stopping this president and his cronies from legalizing over ten million illegal immigrants. To return the favor, these now legal citizens would vote for the party that granted them amnesty. If this should happen, the democrats have essentially bought themselves the white house for many years to come!

Just look at the facts regarding the federal government's refusal to enforce the country's immigration laws. When several states attempted to halt election fraud during the 2012 election by implementing voter-ID laws, the Obama administration sued these states to prevent such actions. When Colorado voted to enforce federal immigration mandates because of the large influx of illegal immigrants breaching their border, Obama's henchmen sued the state to dissuade them. It's mind-blowing that our federal government wishes to abolish voter ID verification requirements when I can't even get a library card or enter a bar without showing my driver's license. The administration's interference in deregulating voter ID is just another ploy to buy votes. The amount of voter fraud during the 2012 presidential election is still unclear, but we have definitive proof that it did exist to some degree. In several voting districts in Cleveland, Ohio, The amount of votes cast during the election exceeded the amount of registered voters in these districts. Obama also stopped construction of the "virtual fence", a seven-hundred mile barrier running along the Mexican-American Border, meant to dissuade the flow of illegal immigrants infiltrating our border.

With one party controlling all facets of our federal government, your personal freedoms and liberties granted under our constitution will surely diminish. The conservative research group, the Heritage Foundation, estimated the expenditures of Obama's first term in office for regulations exceeded $75 seventy-billion.[17] According to a report from the Congress's research arm, the Obama administration's review cycle for pending regulations was longer in 2012 than any point going back to the early 1990s.

Abraham Lincoln once said, *"A house divided against itself cannot stand!"* Our government is the oldest and most successful

---

[17] James L. Gattuso and Diane Katz, "Red Tape Rising: Regulation in Obama's First Term," The Heritage Foundation, May 1, 2013.

form of government in the world today for a reason, because of free-enterprise, not socialism and not big government. Obama's not a stupid man, so asks yourselves why is this man screwing with success?

"President Obama's approval rating is down to 39 percent. And Toronto Mayor Rob Ford, who admitted to smoking crack cocaine, went up to 49 percent. How does this make Obama feel? He'd be better off smoking crack than passing Obamacare." –Jay Leno

Chapter 6

Is Obamacare good for the country?

Senator Max Baucus, one of the chief authors of the Affordable Healthcare Act (Obamacare), recently called the piece of legislation he helped architect as *"an approaching train wreck,"* and The Wall Street Journal, in one of its recent editorials, called Obamacare, *"a fiasco for the ages."* The initial launch of the Obamacare insurance exchange was referred to as an, *"inexcusable mess"* and a *"nightmare"* by USA Today. The cost of Obamacare was originally forecast to reach one trillion dollars over the next ten years. However, current and more accurate projections place the added financial burden much higher than originally estimated, perhaps up to 2.7 trillion a year. Mr. Obama stated that under his plan, insurance premiums would decrease for most, but how is this viable when insurance companies will now incur the added expense of insuring pre-existing conditions and bear the additional costs associated with insuring children below the age of twenty-six still covered under their parent's policy? Also, insurance premiums will rise due to the fact that the Affordable Healthcare Act is a one-size-fits-all plan. The certainty that eighty-five-year-old Mrs. Johnson is required to purchase prenatal, contraceptive, planned-parenthood and pediatric insurance under Obamacare, when she clearly doesn't require such care, only adds unnecessarily to the cost of her insurance premiums. The world's largest health insurer, United Health, recently announced that they are shutting down operations in California due to the supplemental cost of Obamacare, essentially leaving all of their policy-holders in that state without healthcare benefits. United is only one of many insurance companies unable to meet the health standards of the marketplace due to the strict guidelines mandated under Obamacare. It's not like the insurance companies want to cancel the policies of millions of Americans, leaving them without healthcare benefits. So when Obama vilifies the insurance companies for his debacle, remember that it's counterproductive and cost-prohibitive for insurance companies to cancel millions of policy holders and lose billions in future premiums.

As the Affordable Healthcare Act continues its downward death spiral, once again President Obama continues the blame game. This time instead of rebuking the republicans and former president George W. Bush, he now focuses his disparagement on the insurance companies, blaming them for the limitations for yet another failed Obama policy.

Currently about thirty million United States citizens lack healthcare insurance. This is approximately 10% of the population. Under The Affordable Healthcare Act, President Obama estimates that his health plan will cover 95% of the country. So if healthcare benefits will extend to only another 5% of the country's uninsured under his program then aren't there better alternatives than creating a mandated participatory healthcare policy? Can't we come up with an answer to cover the additional 5% of the country without imposing harsh restrictions, penalties and fines? Can't we devise a solution more efficient than caving into the unwavering political agenda of the current administration? Why should the constitutional rights and freedoms of all the citizens of this great nation be discounted to compensate and subsidize a small portion of the population needs? A recent article in Catholic Online outlines a dismal picture on how Obamacare will ultimately degrade the quality of healthcare in this country. The California Medical Association, representing over 100,000 physicians in that state, indicated that 70% of doctors surveyed will opt-out of the Obamacare exchange. Due to Medicaid's new, low reimbursement rates, these doctors can no longer stay in business and turn a profit. Those doctors who don't opt out of the plan may retire altogether.[18]

Not only is the Obamacare exchange website an embarrassment to the administration, but it's filled with glitches and errors. Few people can sign onto the website and even fewer people are able to sign up for government-run health insurance. *Healthcare.com* is riddled with a host of security concerns. The website cost hundreds of millions of dollars to institute and three years to design. However, the initial Obamacare launch was still a colossal failure. Six weeks later, many people are unable to access the web site. Putting aside the fact that only 29,000 people enrolled through the website to date after its initial dismal launch a month and a half ago (meanwhile five million Americans previously covered under private healthcare insurance recently found their current policies canceled

---

[18] Anonomous, "Obamacare crashing in model states like California as 70 percent of doctors opt out," Catholic Online, 12/9/2013.

due to the Obamacare mandates), the website is proving a huge security risk to those who enter their private information on the exchange. There appears no accountability and no precautionary measures taken by the designers of the website to insure the protection of the applicant's private information from "identity theft." When shopping for health insurance through the Obamacare exchange, the website requests a wealth of the applicant's confidential information including, health and sexual history, home address, social security number, financial and credit-card information. Through Obamacare, any dimwitted hacker can infiltrate the system and steal your identity or commit cyber fraud. Identity theft is the largest growing crime in this country. After these criminals and hackers gain access to your personal and private information, they can use this information to destroy your life for many years to come. Once your identity is stolen, it's not like you can run out and get a new one.

In fine print there's a disclaimer under the *Terms & Conditions* provision of the Healthcare.com website which states, "*You have **no reasonable expectation of privacy** regarding any communication or data transiting or stored on this information system. At any time, and for any lawful Government purpose, the government may **monitor,*** *intercept, and search and seize* *any communication or data transiting or stored on this information system. Any communication or data transiting or stored on this information system may be **disclosed or used** for any lawful Government purpose."*[19] This clause denies any culpability on the part of the federal government for compromised information falling into the hands of criminals and hackers. Not only is the government disenfranchising themselves from accountability, but they are telling the American people that they can use our personal information at any time, accessed by any and all unnamed sources in the government, for any reason. Obamacare (which may become the largest database of personal information in the history of our country) will endow the federal government unprecedented knowledge and power over our lives. The Obamacare website is proving a gross violation of our right to privacy. I'm guessing that former presidential candidate Mitt Romney is looking good right about now when he said back in 2012 that his first order of business, after assuming the role of president, was to scrap Obamacare!

---

[19] JERYL BIER, "Obamacare Website Source Code: 'No Reasonable Expectation of Privacy,'
The Weekly Standard, Oct 14, 2013, 12:29 PM.

To add salt to the wound, Health and Human Services Secretary, Kathleen Sebelius, testified recently in front of the Senate Finance Oversight Committee admitting that hackers and convicted felons are eligible candidates as Obamacare navigators. When grilled by Sen. John Cornyn, of Texas, Sebelius revealed under oath that, *"There are no federal requirements for navigators to undergo a criminal background check."* Sebelius went on to further admit, *"States could add in additional background checks and other features, but it is not part of the federal requirement."*[20]

There's a certain irony when a person can't drive a taxi in the country without being fingerprinted and undergoing a thorough background check, but the person privy to my most personal and financial history could have a prior criminal history—or be a convicted murderer for that matter. It's like handing the fox the keys to the chicken coop.

Obamacare is a great benefit for those receiving government subsidies to pay for their healthcare, but for those ineligible to receive

---

[20] Barnini Chakraborty, "Felons could have been hired as ObamaCare 'navigators,' Sebelius tells Senate panel," Fox News Published November 06, 2013

entitlements, we've seen their premiums double and triple. These policy holders are forced to satisfy large deductibles of $6,000, $12,000 or more before coverage actually kicks in. Current estimates forecast that under Obamacare's individual mandate, fifteen million responsible tax-paying people will eventually lose their current health plans to cover those uninsured and people who don't work for a living. The insurance companies are forced to drop coverage for many because of the AHC one-size-fits-all requirements, and the fact that their policies don't meet Obamacare standards. This is contradictory to Mr. Obama's previous assertions that, *"If you like your current health plan and your current doctors, you can keep your current health plan and your current doctors."* We now know that Mr. Obama had prior knowledge going back to 2010 that many people would lose their current healthcare policies under Obamacare, but the president kept up the façade and deferred the employer healthcare mandate until the end of 2014. He lied and deceived the American people so that he could increase his 2012 reelection chances and pass Obamacare. If he was initially honest back in 2010 with the American people and explained that a good portion of them would lose their private healthcare due to the new government mandates, do you really think anyone would have supported the plan?

The Supreme Court's ruling to uphold Obamacare shows the level of their corruption and incompetence. Since when is it legal to mandate an individual to buy into a program where their premiums increase and where the IRS has unrestrained power to fine and imprison noncompliance? Where is the virtue in allowing the IRS executive privilege to obtain a wealth of an individual's financial and health-related information? That the IRS can then use this information to incriminate the American people? We've already seen how the IRS used privileged information to target and discriminate against conservative Tea Party groups attempting to apply for tax-exempt status. Back in 2010, the IRS either placed a "hold" on or denied altogether the requests for these conservative groups applying for tax-exemption during this time period. Sir John Dalberg-Acton once said, *"Power tends to corrupt, and absolute power corrupts absolutely."* Knowledge is power and we've already seen how the IRS used this power to harm others.

Obamacare will ultimately force employers to take on the added burden of a larger portion of their worker's exploding insurance premiums. These companies in turn will most likely either downsize their workforce in order to prevent bankruptcy, hindering job growth and job creation or be forced to transfer some of the plan's increased financial responsibilities to their employees. Companies like, Subway and Wendy's are cutting hours, while Papa Johns is increasing the price of their pizzas to compensate for the added healthcare costs. Many companies like UPS are now refusing to pay for spousal healthcare benefits because of Obamacare. A large percentage of businesses are geared towards laying off workers or restrict the number of their employee's hours to recompose for the thirty-hour work week threshold instituted under the provisions of the Affordable Healthcare Act. Not only are businesses harshly affected by the new law, but cities, townships, hospitals and schools are also reducing hours or laying off our policemen, firemen, paramedics, teachers and nurses. This is the case of the state of Ohio's second largest employer, the Cleveland Clinic. They are considering laying off an alarming portion of their 44,000 employees. These cuts are deemed necessary to comply with the Obamacare mandates and simultaneously remain solvent. Sea World recently dropped their employees' hours to accommodate a mandated twenty-eight-hour work week. Also, Obamacare encourages the depression of the housing market. If a homeowner is successful in selling their property in today's lackluster economy, under the provisions of Obamacare, the seller is hit with a 2% estate tax. So, if your house sells for $250,000, you're forced to give the federal government $5,000 in additional taxes right off the bat. With unemployment hovering over 8% for the last five straight years, can we really afford to lose more jobs in this already volatile economy? Although not always affordable to all, The United States has the best healthcare in the world. Why not focus our efforts on reducing the costs of this healthcare without jeopardizing the quality of care? Under Obamacare jobs decrease and so do wages.

Contrary to Mr. Obama's fallacious promise about the benefits of Obamacare, according to well renowned healthcare economist, Christopher Conover, "Out of the 189 million Americans currently covered by private healthcare, sixty-eight percent of the policy holders will potentially lose their current plan by the end of 2014 and twenty to fifty million Americans may lose their healthcare altogether."[21] Outlined by a recent report

---

[21] Jamie Weinstein, The Dailey Caller, "Expert: At least 129 million will 'not be able to keep' health care plan if Obamacare fully implemented," 12:45 AM 11/04/2013

published by the Government Accountability Office it's estimated that our current debt will rise another six trillion dollars due to Obamacare.

In the wake of millions of Americans losing their privately-held insurance policies due to the new healthcare bill, the president recently met with the CEOs of large insurance companies. He petitioned them to reinstate the individual policies that were recently revoked. The move will essentially collapse Obamacare, because those reinstated will no longer be required to purchase health insurance through the Obamacare exchange. Obamacare relies on these premiums to keep the program solvent. It's taken the insurance companies over three years at the cost of many millions of dollars to adjust their rates and rewrite their policies to comply with the Obamacare mandates. Even if the insurance companies wanted to restore the original policies in the wake of the Obamacare implosion, it's not a quick-fix from a logistics standpoint. Not only is restoring the policies time-consuming and costly, but why would these insurance companies spend all that energy and expense to reinstitute policies that are scheduled to expire and revert back to Obamacare directives by next October? I think that the federal government is once again insulting the intelligence of the American people by announcing the delay of the small-business Obamacare mandates until two weeks after the 2014 elections. The White House is essentially hoping that the American people are "too stupid" to realize the cataclysmic detrimental repercussions that Obamcare is causing on our already fragile economy. The president is attempting to improve the democrat's chances of capturing the House before everyone wakes up and sees the Obamacare disaster for the farce it really is. Does an ethical guy delay a problem so that his party can maintain power while deceiving the people they govern or does a virtuous person tackle the problems head-on regardless of the future outcome?

If Barak Obama is attempting to steer the country towards socialism, wouldn't Obamacare be the perfect instrument for implementing this ideology? The new healthcare act would force many businesses to downsize, leaving millions of people without employment. The government would then step in and support these people through entitlement programs and thus control the masses. It's a perfect scheme. Many would argue that Obamacare is nothing more than an insidious instrument devised to control the masses. It's a convoluted piece of legislation whose bill was never reviewed by the president nor any democrat in Congress, but gives the federal government greater increased control over our lives. With the incorporation of Obamacare, 16,000 new IRS agents were hired to monitor, regulate, and penalize non-compliance. The executive branch will have unprecedented access to a wealth of an individual's personal information. The fact that Obama recently used the IRS to target and attack conservative opposition party members is a prime example of the impending abuse of this knowledge.

During a 2012 Socrates Club Debate at the University of Oregon, conservative political commentator and former college professor, Dinesh Dsouza, gave a compelling argument addressing Obamacare from an "integrity" standpoint. Arguing against universal healthcare, he broke down the implications of "morality" using a "sandwich" as a metaphor. Mr. Dsouza claimed that if Peter had a sandwich and Paul was hungry, Peter can offer Paul the sandwich and the exchange is a morally beneficial transaction between both parties. Peter feels content and rewarded because he gave the sandwich to help Paul without proclamation, and Paul is nourished and satisfied because Peter donated the sandwich under his own free accord. Paul feels no guilt or regret for accepting the endowment. Now along comes Obama riding on his white horse wielding a gun. He jumps off the horse and holds the gun to Peter's head, forcing peter to give up the sandwich to Paul. The results are the same because Paul now possesses the sandwich, but the moral implications are far different. Peter feels angry and discontent because his sandwich was coerced from his possession and his offering was insincere. He can't take the moral high-ground since the sandwich wasn't sacrificed out of the goodness of his heart. Paul doesn't feel grateful for receiving the sandwich, but rather feels a sense of entitlement. He now wants more sandwiches.

One may conclude that it's necessary for Obama to hold a gun to Peter's head because Peter isn't a moral person and won't extend Paul the sandwich without coercion. Obama may claim himself a charitable and commendable individual, but the reality is that Obama pointing the gun at Peter is equally as immoral as Peter refusing to relinquish the sandwich. Obama may toot his own horn, claiming credit for a moral and just act, but the fact remains that the sandwich wasn't Obama's to begin with and it certainly wasn't his to give away. Before the launching of the Affordable Healthcare Act back in October, many people were excited about the premise of receiving free or affordable healthcare, but the reality is that Obamacare is an insidious piece of legislation designed to literally steal from Peter to pay Paul.

Mr. Dsouza conceded that there are members in every culture who are disabled and need assistance from the rest of society. It's Mr. Dsouza's personal opinion that roughly 10% of society usually requires some sort of government assistance in order to survive. Under Obama's watch, the county's entitlement programs are growing exponentially. Mr. Dsouza presented a compelling argument about the correlation between Obamacare and the moral destruction of society by using a "wagon" as a metaphor. He claims that the rest of society must pull the wagon filled with society's needy and take up the slack for those who can't support themselves. However, under the Obama administration, a greater number of people are jumping into the wagon. As the number of people riding in the wagon exceeds the number of people pulling the wagon, the pulling of the wagon becomes more tedious and cumbersome. Likewise, when the people pulling the wagon see what a raw deal they are getting, they too will also want to jump on the band wagon.

Obama demonizes and demoralizes the people pulling the wagon. He calls the wagon-pullers selfish, greedy and materialistic. In reality, it is these altruistic martyrs of society who bear the load for the rest of us. If the wagon-pullers decide that they won't pull the wagon anymore, then the wagon stops moving and so does our economy. Likewise, if more people jump in the wagon and there are no longer enough wagon-pullers, the wagon ends up getting stuck in the mud. Obama doesn't give credit where credit is due.

Contrary to the White House's claims that the republicans don't have a comprehensive and legitimate program geared at revamping our antiquated healthcare structure, the party is dedicated to healthcare reform. Both democratic and republican congressional leaders alike agree that the "status quo" for maintaining our current healthcare system is ineffectual and unacceptable. Under the republican plan, called *The Empowered Patients First Act*, instead of the government running the entire healthcare system, the private insurance market is opened up and expanded. By taking advantage of our free-market structure, liberties and responsibilities are given to the individual to select policies catered to their own individual needs. Instead of the "one-size-fits-all"

Obamacare prescription, the republicans feel that by allowing individuals to shop for health insurance on a country-wide basis (instead of only through their respective states), insurance premiums and deductibles will automatically decrease. Republicans believe that by pooling resources and taking advantage of the free-market the shift will break up state-controlled insurance monopolies and increase competition leading to more affordable and flexible health plans. The policy also calls for individual tax credits to reimburse out-of-pocket medical expenses and extends tax incentives for individuals and employers for promoting "healthy-living" choices. Doctors are reimbursed for extending preventive-care and optimal-care. Physicians will also receive government subsidies for refusing to discriminate against patients with pre-existing conditions. The health costs for these pre-existing conditions are mitigated due to the large pooling mechanisms in place. Since the healthcare system is privatized, the republican plan will not add to the federal deficit because it doesn't draw from the federal budget. This is contrary to the conservative estimates of $2.7 trillion that the Obamacare is expected to add to our debt over the next several years. Do you think that the government has a better idea of you and your family's healthcare needs or do you feel that you should decide what healthcare is best for you and your family?

Excuse me if I'm a little skeptical whether our government will run an efficient and cost-effective healthcare system. It's not like they haven't already bankrupted a great deal of the programs currently under their supervision! Medicaid and Medicare are broke, Social Security is broke, the United States Post Office is broke, our military is on the brink of being downsized to the smallest levels since World War I through sequestration and besides Obama using NASA to research "Muslim outreach" do we even have a space program anymore? So if you put your faith in a successful government-run healthcare system, just look at how poorly our federal government has decimated other programs of the same caliber under their stewardship.

In the 2012 presidential debates, Barak Obama said that we have to reelect him to see his grand plan fully realized. That we can't quit now and to stay the course. What exactly does this plan entail? His strategy for a new America is starting to scare the hell out of me and mine. This far-left liberal ideology that big government is the answer to all our problems is a sham. Big government is bureaucratic and inefficient. It does not work to the scope

Obama wants it to… period! You think Obamacare is a mess now, just wait until the employer mandate kicks in at the end of 2014. The reality is that Obamacare is an insolvent program that remains afloat (at least for the time being) by deficit spending.

According to Godfather Politics, Obamacare contains roughly twenty new taxes effecting the middle class, seniors on fixed incomes and the members of the lower class—despite Obama's broken pledge not to raise taxes and his promise to reduce the costs of our healthcare. The implication is that the economy's financial collapse will set the stage for Obama's complete takeover.[22] When George Bush Senior back in 1992 lost his reelection bid because of a 1988 broken promise not to raise taxes—he said, *Read my lips: no new taxes!*—why shouldn't we hold this current president accountable for the same broken promise!

---

[22] Da Tagliare, "Thousands Losing Jobs Due to Obamacare," Godfather Politics, November 12, 2012

The average citizen finds his orderly world eroding or even crumbling beneath his feet. His savings have recently become a very slippery kind of security. Taxes, inflation, and high interest rates are ravenously gnawing away at his dwindling standard of living. His hopes of a pleasant and safe retirement are proving illusionary. He has a feeling that he is being propagandized, programmed and over-governed to the point where his personal freedom seems to be shrinking on all fronts.

–W. Cleon Skousen

Chapter 7

Are we better off than we were five years ago?

Looking across the board, has any particular individual socioeconomic class really thrived from the Obama policies? The number of those impoverished has grown out of control. Since Obama first took office we have eighteen million more people collecting food stamps. Food stamp expenditures have currently exceeded seventy-five billion dollars a year. Six million people are collecting extended unemployment benefits and there are another five million people on welfare. Our entitlement programs are bursting at the seams, growing to their greatest levels in our nation's history. As a matter of fact, forty-nine million Americans received some sort of government assistance last year. As our federal government continues to increase our civilians' dependency on government creating a "nanny state", this will increase voters' allegiance to the particular political party handing out these "freebies." In this case it's Obama and the democrats. During the 2012 election presidential candidate, Mitt Romney made a statement behind closed doors that 47% of the people weren't going to vote for him. Mr. Romney was harshly criticized in the liberal media for his off-the-cusp remark, but if you look at the facts, what he was saying was spot-on. Whether you need government assistance or whether you're only exploiting the system, in the words of Rush Limbaugh, *"You're not going to vote against Santa Claus."*

The current administration's harsh regulatory policies are hindering our industry leaders from hiring and growing the economy, but perhaps the one group hit the hardest by the president's failed agenda is the backbone of America, its middle class. The average median annual income of those making $55,000 or less has plummeted nearly $4,500 dollars since

2008. The cost of living is up, but wages are stagnant. The average period for unemployment between jobs is nearly forty weeks. This is up from twenty weeks under the Bush administration. The average prices of gas, milk and bread have all doubled since Obama first took office and even though most college students voted for Mr. Obama in the last election, college tuition has risen dramatically since 2008.

Obama's policies are bad for the United States, period! The warped ideology of taking from those who've earned it and giving to those who don't deserve it is setting a dangerous precedence. Do you think it's fair that 50% of the country pays 100% of our expenditures? That's right, 50% of our country doesn't pay income tax. One of Mitt Romney's campaign promises was to decrease the tax burden of the middle class. Why should someone not currently paying taxes care whether someone paying taxes gets a tax break? This is selfish thinking on the part of many. After all, in the long-run we either thrive as a country or we falter as a country. Under the Obama policies I don't think it's ethical or honorable to ask those footing the entire bill to pay more. This kind of egocentric thinking is not conducive to a successful democracy and sets a bad example.

The National Commission on Fiscal Responsibility and Reform often referred to as Simpson-Bowls was an outreach program administered by the Obama administration to help cultivate the economy. The commission and its findings were supported by a majority of its members, including both democrats and republicans as well as the CEO of Morgan Stanley. The White House however failed to implement the plan, which tackled the issues of reducing our debt and stabilizing our economy. Critics of the proposal argued that it would force a reduction in entitlement programs. Since Obama doesn't want to touch on the subject of entitlement reform, he ignored the Simpson-Bowls findings altogether.

I deem it unlawful that President Obama is attempting to grant amnesty to all illegal immigrants currently residing in our country. If you want to go through the legal proceedings to become a citizen of the United States like past generations, I commend these actions, but to give illegal immigrants social security and healthcare benefits that I've been paying into since I was eleven years old, upsets me to no end. Rewarding apathy and discouraging success and hard work is anti-American. This country prospers from entrepreneurial thinkers and risk-takers, not an over-imposing, over-bearing, over-inflated government. So the next time Al Sharpton protests racial discord, I argue that the only group of people truly being discriminated against in our country today is our struggling middle class. It's the middle class that bears the brunt of Obama's failed policies and radical agenda. Under this administration, the annual income tax rate rose 5%, the payroll tax surged 15%, capital gains tax has nearly doubled and the estate tax jumped from 0% to 55%. To prove that the middle class is being hammered nowadays, 43% of all American households are currently spending more each year than they are earning and a recent CBS morning show claimed that 76% of all families in this country live paycheck to paycheck. The middle class is the rock—they are the source of America's greatness and to turn our backs on them now would do our country a great disservice.

As a country, we're certainly not better off than we were five years ago. The overwhelming ominous statistics paint a dismal picture. The federal debt is currently 67% of GDP and the federal spending is a whopping 25% of GDP. These are the highest totals since World War II. Unemployment is so high that only 58% of the country is currently working (the lowest total since The Great Depression). Long-term unemployment has reached monumental proportions and is the highest since the 1930s. In fact, only 49% of the country paid income tax last year. This is the lowest percentage in the modern era. Under this president, those receiving government aid also rose to 45%. This figure is also the highest in our history, while homeownership is down to its lowest level since the 1960s. We've experienced the lowest job growth and the slowest job market recovery in our country since the Second World War. From 2003 to 2008, under a republican controlled Congress, jobs grew by almost two million, but while under a democratic leadership since 2008 we lost eight million jobs.

"Whoever is careless with the truth in small matters cannot be trusted with important matters"

- Albert Einstein

Chapter 8

Is Obama a nice guy?

When I asked people why they voted for Obama in the last election, many of them exclaimed that he is a nice guy. For me, the most telling insight into the morality of our fearless leader emerged the morning after the attack on our consulate in Benghazi by radical Islamic militants. The Al-Qaeda affiliated terrorists, wielding rocket propelled grenades, ignited our embassy, murdering Ambassador Chris Stevens and three others. The slaying of Ambassador Stevens marked the first time in nearly thirty-five years that a United States Ambassador was murdered while in office. Even though the assault was clearly an "act of terrorism" based on the evidence that the well-organized assailants were heavily armed, the White House refused to label it as such. The administration called the unprovoked attack "a spontaneous uprising." An act of terrorism on American soil didn't play into their narrative that Al-Qaeda was on the decline. Conceding an act of terrorism would deprecate Mr. Obama's only crowning achievement for his first four years as president—killing Osama Bin Laden. With an election coming up, the administration couldn't afford to acknowledge that terrorism was on the rise.

This is also why the White House down-played Nidal Malik Hasan's premeditated slaying of thirteen innocent people at Fort Hood. They labeled the slaughter, "workplace violence" instead of the ruthless terror attack it was, even after Hasan expressed deep anti-American sentiment. The administration blamed this blatant Libyan terrorist attack in Benghazi on an anti-Muslim YouTube video that most Americans never viewed and which the US Government had no affiliation with. Nearly a week after the Benghazi raid, President Obama appeared on *The View* where he continued blaming the video for the attack. However, he disclosed to television host, Joy Behar that the investigation was still ongoing and we shouldn't jump to conclusions until all the facts in the case were brought to light. We now know the White House had real-time feeds of the events as they unfolded. We knew it was terrorism from the very beginning so why blame a video? Obama refrained from making a formal statement, but sent then US Ambassador Susan Rice to the United Nations on five separate morning shows only hours after the assault. She blamed the attack on the YouTube video to divert attention. The White House had real-time knowledge of the events as they occurred, but refused to help save our people. The only person who was ever demoted or lost their job over the Benghazi fiasco was State Department official, Raymond Maxwell, who tried to tell the truth about what really happened during the night of the raid. Maxwell was singled out for disciplinary action even though The State Department's Office of Internal Affairs admitted that they didn't find a reasonable semblance of "misconduct" committed on the part of Mr. Maxwell. In fact, without congressional approval and after all of her lies and erroneous talking points, Susan Rice was promoted to National Security Advisor. If Ms. Rice didn't have the support of the current administration when she appeared on those talks shows dispersing blame for the Benghazi affair on an internet video and if her actions were contrary to the thoughts and views of our president—then why promote her?

It doesn't make sense that the White House didn't have prior knowledge of Susan Rice's talking points. Former Lybian president, Muammar Gaddafi, professed the attack on elements of Ansar al-Sharia for the slayings, linking them to Al-Qaeda in the Islamic Maghreb region. Gaddafi was murdered in an uprising soon after. We have clues leading to those responsible for the attack in Benghazi, but no guilty parties were ever apprehended in the slayings and it doesn't even seem like we are still looking for the culprits. How is it possible to gain a foothold on our fight against terrorism if our government can't even admit terrorism exists?

Abigail Van Buren (Dear Abby) once said, *"The best index to a person's character is how he treats people who can't do him any good, and how he treats people who can't fight back."* Hours after the Benghazi attack, our Commander in Chief hopped a flight on Air Force One to Las Vegas for a campaign fundraiser. Here is a guy sworn to protect the American people home and abroad and he was more selfishly concerned about campaigning for re-election. He and his committee for re-elect harshly criticized candidate Romney for making a prompt statement to the press condemning the attack, but Obama didn't offer his own response until seventeen hours after the fact. When he finally tendered a statement, Mr. Obama blamed the attack on a video. As a matter of fact, Mr. Obama and his committee to reelect chastised Mitt Romney for his expedient comments quicker and more harshly than the Benghazi terrorists themselves. I don't know about you, but I like a leader who is proactive and protects the interests of the American people, not a leader who bows before and apologizes to the heads of middle-eastern countries for any ill-will between our nations. If someone burned down my house and slaughtered my family, the last thing on my mind would be apologizing to the bastards responsible, yet that's exactly what our executive branch did.

Following the attack we spent seventy-five million taxpayer dollars running ads in Pakistan apologizing for the American way-of-life. In November of 2012, then Secretary of State, Hillary Clinton, apologized to the Pakistani Government for the deaths of two-dozen Pakistani soldiers killed during a border clash. We gave their country $1.3 billion in foreign aid after they hid the world's most notorious terrorist from us for all those years. It's never been proven that the Pakistani Government had prior knowledge of Bin Laden's whereabouts. However, it's highly suspect that they didn't know of his location due to the fact that the prestigious Pakistan Military Academy at Kakul is located less than a mile from the former Bin Laden compound. It seems unlikely that Bin Laden wouldn't seek sanctuary in Pakistan all those years if he didn't feel safe and protected there. By the way, Obama frequently totes his achievement of executing the world's most notorious villain, but I argue any sitting president would have given executive orders to pull that trigger. Hell, I'm convinced that George W. Bush wanted Osama so badly, he'd probably would have hopped on a flight to Pakistan and pulled the trigger himself if given the opportunity. It was the infamous water-boarding techniques started under Bush and banned by Obama, which led to the intelligence responsible for Bin Laden's ultimate capture. Although Mr. Obama took credit for the killing, in reality it was our Navy SEALS who were responsible for the success of the mission. Obama repaid these brave men by publically revealing to the world their true identities. Is it any surprise that soon after the disclosure twenty-two members of SEAL Team Six—the group directly responsible for carrying out the Bin Laden raid—were killed when their helicopter was shot down by two Taliban jets? It was the largest loss of human life in the history of the Navy's Special Forces Division.

Does a nice guy brag about killing people? According to a new book by journalists, Mark Halperin and John Heilemann, called *Double-Down*, President

Obama bragged to staffers when discussing drone strikes that he's "really good at killing people." Is this the same president who won the Nobel **PEACE** Prize?

In the wake of the Benghazi tragedy, when asked why President Obama didn't cancel his trip to Las Vegas, one of his chief campaign strategists said that if Mitt Romney and Paul Ryan didn't suspend campaigning efforts than why should they. I found this statement utterly appalling. Mr. Obama, our Commander in Chief, sworn to protect the American way of life home and abroad, was more narcissistically concerned about promoting his reelection chances than investigating the attack. Soon after Representative, Paul Ryan coined Obama the nickname, *"Campaigner and Chief."*

Mr. Obama spent most of 2012 focusing on getting reelected. As a matter of fact, Mr. Obama's first term reelection campaigns exceeded the combined totals of Jimmy Carter, Both Bushes, Clinton and Reagan. Obama attended over one hundred and ninety fund raisers during this time. That's one fund raiser a day for six months straight!

Obama campaign spokeswoman, Stephanie Cutter told Fox News analyst, Bret

Bair that Romney and Ryan were politicizing the Benghazi affair to gain support for their campaign, because of Romney's reprimanding response the morning after the Benghazi attack. She said that was the job of our president yet our president was unresponsive. Does anyone recall that Stephanie Cutter is the same person who accused Mitt Romney of the death of the wife of a GTS Steel employee, even though Romney left Bain Capital years before this woman died of cancer? Bain was involved with the closing of GTS. After the company was phased out, Cutter attempted to tie Romney to the family's loss of health insurance and the woman's subsequent death from cancer.

Mr. Obama spent the entire 2012 election attacking the character of his opponent, never disavowing himself from egregious campaign ads and outlandish accusations. Ads that claimed the conservatives promoted programs geared towards "dirty air" and "dirty water" for our children. That republicans wanted to push a wheelchair-bound granny off the cliff. That Romney was a tax-cheat, when this was proven the contrary. I can't recall any moments during the presidential debates or through campaign ads that focused on our economic recovery. There were no solutions generated by our president, only threats against his opponents. It was like he was telling the American people that he was the better of the two evils. A major reason why Romney failed in his quest for the presidency was because he refused to stoop to his opponent's level and castigate the incumbent. Romney lost because his message no longer holds value with the American people. Reducing taxes, creating jobs, promoting businesses and free-enterprise have taken a back-seat to receiving "free stuff." This is why during the 2012 election the president never had to offer a second term agenda or defend his first-term failures. We as a nation shouldn't settle, we deserve better. We should elect a leader willing to help us grow and prosper. Only when Romney came out with a laundry list of ways on improving the economy did Obama come out with his ridiculous "seven-point plan." Have we heard anything more about this "seven-point plan" since Obama got reelected? As a matter of fact, Mr. Obama has failed to pass a single national budget as president. Not only has he failed to pass a comprehensive cohesive federal budget while in office, but not a solitary member of Congress, including the democrats, voted to approve any of his plans. How can our government effectively manage our country if they can't even pass a budget and balance their own checkbook?

Obama said the republican policies for recovery didn't add up and Romney would hike up taxes to the tune of five trillion dollars, decimating the middle class. His claims were unsubstantiated because his opponent intended to close loopholes for society's most affluent. Meanwhile, Obama offered no sound solutions of his own for reducing our bulging national debt or implementing programs geared at curbing our entitlement programs. We now see that Obama is the one raising taxes to monumental levels. Obamacare will eventually end up raping the middle class, imposing the highest taxes ever (18 new taxes in all)! Is it any wonder that more Americans are renouncing their US citizenship due to the increased tax burden? The Wall Street Journal recently reported that the expatriations level grew to a record 33% this year.[23]

Obama pledged back in 2008 that his presidency would be the most transparent in

---

[23] Laura Saunders, "More Taxpayers Are Abandoning the U.S.," The Wall Street Journal, Nov. 13, 2013 1:15 p.m. ET.

our nation's history, yet his time in office is racked with more scandals (most of them impeachable offenses) and more secrecy then any of his predecessors. President Nixon resigned before impeachment hearings were initiated because of the Watergate break-in. It's ironic that President Nixon was forced to resign before impeachments proceedings for bugging his opponents, but when this current sitting president uses the National Security Agency (NSA) to spy on millions of Americans, this highly unethical and criminal act is overlooked by the entire country. Watergate was Tiddlywinks compared to the two dozen scandals this president is involved with. Fast & Furious, Solyndra, ACORN, using the IRS to intimidate conservative opponents, Benghazi, using the NSA to spy on Americans, raising our debt to unsustainable levels and mortgaging our children's future, creating a "kill list" granting executive order to authorize the killing of Americans home and abroad and promoting widespread voter fraud to name a few. The ignominy list goes on and on and yet the lapdog liberal media and our complacent society refuse to hold this president accountable for his egregious transgressions. Obama promised to end lobbyists in Washington, yet under his watch lobbyists and special-interest groups have grown substantially. Union delegates and affiliates were invited to the White House more than any other private sector group during the last five years. In fact, some union officials engage the president more often than many of the his cabinet members. Union dues collectively reach billions of dollars each year and a good portion of this money is allotted to campaign contributions. Unions in this country now have more power than ever, killing job growth and undermining education. If you can't fire an ineffectual teacher, then how does this help the student? As a matter of fact, in an unscrupulous attempt to appease Obama's labor union buddies for their millions of dollars in donations they endowed to push through Obamacare, the president is exempting "certain self-insured unions" from paying the requirement tax penalties in 2015 and 2016. Isn't it convenient that the unions who pushed for Obamacre as well as the president and Congress who voted the bill into law, exempted themselves from the plan? Who do you think will now take up the burden and get stuck paying for the added cost of those exempted? You guessed it, Joe Q. Public!

Does a nice guy take God out of the equation? During the 2012 Democratic

Convention, the inference to God, our creator, was purposefully and methodically removed from the democratic platform. Quickly realizing their mistake, when attempting to reinstitute our nation's dedication to God, the attending delegates "booed" the reinstatement. How can this administration disrespect our Heavenly Father? God is a very intricate part of our infrastructure. *"In God we trust,"* is on our currency. In The Pledge of Allegiance, we say *"One nation, Under GOD, Indivisible, for Liberty and Justice for all."* Under our Declaration of Independence it reads: *"We hold these truths to be self-evident, that all men are created equal, that they are endowed by their **Creator** with certain unalienable Rights that among these are Life, Liberty and the pursuit of Happiness."* When reciting this passage, during numerous occasions, Mr. Obama intentionally misquotes our nation's most cherished symbol of independence by leaving out key words from its passages. Instead of saying, *"...are endowed by their Creator with certain unalienable rights,"* or president frequently recites, *"...are endowed with certain unalienable rights."*

It's amazing that this administration infringes upon the civil rights of our catholic churches by forcing them to include free contraceptives in their health plans—it's beleaguering that the president intentionally snubbed Israel Prime Minister, Benjamin Netanyahu when the Jewish leader and one of our greatest allies demanded a conference to discuss the impending Iran nuclear crisis (Obama had more pressing obligations attending Jay Z's party in the Hamptons and appearing on David Letterman). It's also obscene that our dedication to Israel was intentionally removed from the opening speech of the democratic convention. Yet, our president can't wait to bow before and make concessions to Islamic sultans and apologize to Muslims for our values and ethnic diversity. Now isn't the time to turn our backs on God. John 3:36 states, *"He who believes in the Son has everlasting life: and he who does not believe the Son shall not see life, but the wrath of God abides him."* It bothers me and many Americans that this sitting president is the only president in our history that intentionally failed to place his hand on the Bible while swearing the oath of office. What will happen if we turn our backs on God when we now need him more than ever? God works through faith. This isn't the time for us as a nation to abandon our faith.

"Nearly all men can stand adversity, but if you want to test a man's character, give him power."

- Abraham Lincoln

Chapter 9

Is the federal government trying to control your life?

Ray Bradbury's 1959 classic dystopian novel, *Fahrenheit 451* deals with government censorship and Big Brother's attempt to suppress dissention by those opposed to their bureaucratic ideologies. In this literary masterpiece firemen were used to incinerate all books and written works contradictory to government views. It is a devious plot to control the masses by keeping the populace ignorant and uniformed.

Over the last five years, we've seen our constitutional rights and freedoms continually infringed upon by the current administration. There are many examples outlining the numerous infractions and illicit transactions opposing the mandates of the constitution. Back in 2009 President Obama was elected to

Chairman of the U.N. Security Council. This is a highly unprecedented and illegal maneuver prohibited under article 1.9 within our constitution, which bans any US-elected official from maintaining a foreign office or holding a foreign title. The reasoning behind this constitutional provision is to prevent foreign influence from American Internal Affairs.[24] We already saw that during the 2012 presidential election the United Nations attempted to monitor the presidential polls in Texas (coincidentally the largest conservative state in the union). The move prompted Texas Attorney General, Greg Abbot, to send a letter warning the United Nation would-be poll observers that they do not have jurisdiction in Texas and will, therefore, be criminally prosecuted if they attempt to interfere at Texas polling. The United Nations also overstepped their authority when they tried to impose a world-wide tax on the internet. Imagine having to pay a surtax every time you surf a web site.

Article 1.1 of the constitution expressly prohibits our executive branch from appointing

---

[24] Scotty Starnes, "How has Obama Violated the Constitution? Let's Count the Ways," Politically Incorrect Conservative, January 2, 2011.

czars. The president may appoint managers, but these appointees are expressly forbidden under our constitution from possessing any regulatory and law-making authority. These powers are reserved exclusively for our legislative branch. The number for appointees who now report directly to the president has reached monumental proportions. This type of political structure is frighteningly similar to communist Russia. Today's "czars" are not vetted by Congress. They aren't elected officials (so they're not bound to report to Congress), but possess unlimited legal and political decision-making power.[25]

Under Article 1.2 of the constitution, our executive branch doesn't have the authority to selectively give tax rebates to individuals for specific purchases like automobiles. This didn't stop President Obama from enacting the Cash for Clunkers Program, where specific individuals could trade in their old car and get a tax rebate for purchasing a new one. The six billion dollar blunder had no measurable influence on our economic recovery and only

---

[25] Scotty Starnes, Politically Incorrect Conservative, January 2, 2011.

served to get people in further debt by allowing these individuals to accrue another loan.[26]

The 2008 Tarp Act was another gross violation of the constitution. Article 1.8 prohibits Congress from diverting funds to specific organizations or institutions. However, by executive order, the stimulus bill provided a seven hundred billion dollar bail-out loan to big banks and insurance companies. Congress nor the president has the authority to endow individual companies access to federal loans.[27] Likewise, once a bill is signed into law, the president doesn't have the legal authority to unilaterally grant waivers and exemptions to specific individuals and corporations.

When Colorado attempted to control the influx of illegal immigrants breaching their borders, our federal government sued the state to prevent them from upholding the existing federal immigration law and impeded the state's ability to secure its boundaries.

Fast & Furious, a government gun-tracking program aimed at stemming the illegal

---

[26] Scotty Starnes, Politically Incorrect Conservative, January 2, 2011

[27] Scotty Starnes, Politically Incorrect Conservative, January 2, 2011

flow of firearms to Mexico was an embarrassment to the Attorney General's Office and the Justice Department. The program blew up in the administration's face when border patrolman, Brian Terry, was murdered by a band of drug smugglers illegally crossing into the United States. The weapon responsible for Terry's death was traced back to the Fast & Furious Program. The Bureau of Alcohol, Tobacco, Firearms and Explosives, responsible for managing the program, allowed thousands of illegal weapons to fall into the hands of Mexican drug cartels and crime syndicates. Agent Terry was murdered by a member of Mexico's *Sinaloa* drug cartel. It was later revealed that The Bureau of Alcohol, Tobacco, Firearms and Explosives intentionally allowed the sale of over 2,000 guns to suspected criminals linked to Mexican drug gangs. It was part of an ongoing investigation to infiltrate the Mexican drug hierarchy. The incompetence with the program was revealed when the ATF lost track of the weapons, evident by the fact that two of the guns registered through the program turned up at the Terry crime scene. Attempting to shield the Obama Administration from any embarrassment in the matter, Attorney General, Eric Holder, refused to disclose pertinent documents related in the case to the House congressional oversight committee. Mr. Holder continually lied and perjured himself when questioned about the facts in the case and was eventually indicted for contempt of Congress on both felony and civil charges. Mr. Holder is the first and only ever sitting cabinet member held in contempt for both civil and criminal misconduct. With things heating up for Holder, Obama asserted his "executive privilege" burying the documents and sparring Holder from the gallows. So much for the self-proclaimed most transparent presidency in our history.

Just this week *The New York Post* ran a story that back in 2012, several months before the presidential election, the Census Bureau fudged the unemployment figures from 8.1% to 7.8%. The move was significant because it allowed Obama to toot his own horn inferring that his policies for economic recovery were working. This was in strong contrast to Romney's assertions that under Obama leadership our country suffered from "economic paralysis" and an "anemic recovery." The unemployment rate is a strong indicator of our economic stability. The deception placed Obama in a much stronger position to regain the White House, because it made Romney's proclamation look unfounded. It was a nefarious criminal act designed to specifically mislead the American people.

Wasn't it Henry Kissinger who once said, *"Corrupt politicians make the other ten percent look bad?"*

Obamacare is without a doubt the grossest violation of our civil rights granted under the constitution and our greatest injustice. The program is nothing more than a redistribution of wealth from the "responsible" to the "irresponsible". The law mandates citizens to purchase healthcare whether they want it or not. Federal Judge Henry E. Hudson recently said that the federal government has no power "to compel an individual to involuntarily enter the stream of commerce by purchasing a commodity in the private market."[28] The constitution also specifically prohibits any changes or amendments by an individual after a bill is signed into law. However, after Obamacare was enacted, our president opted to grant illegal executive privileges by displaying partiality and exempting specific individuals and agencies from participating in the mandate.

In the wake of the collapse of Obamacare, as premiums are skyrocketing and

---

[28] Rosalind S. Helderman and Amy Goldstein, "Federal judge in Va. strikes down part of health-care law," The Washington Post Blog, Tuesday, December 14, 2010; 12:49 AM

people are dropped from their existing plans, the president stands firm on his assurances that his healthcare plan will succeed once the kinks are worked out. He compares his program to the successful Massachusetts healthcare act incorporated by then Governor Mitt Romney. Obama said that his plan is the same plan as "Romneycare." Mr. Romney recently debunked the correlations between the two plans, Tweeting, "The years since the Massachusetts health care law went into effect nothing has changed my view that a plan crafted to fit the unique circumstances of a single state should not be grafted onto the entire country." My Romney went on to further comment that, "Health reform is best crafted by states with bipartisan support and input from its employers, as we did, without raising taxes, and by carefully phasing it in to avoid the type of disruptions we are seeing nationally."

Another unethical and incontestable example of government suppression is apparent by the fact that the White House instituted three separate surveillance web sites geared at monitoring ill content towards the administration. In order to spy on the masses, the White House developed a web site called Flag@Whitehouse.gov, which was implemented to encourage fellow Americans to squeal on those spreading inflammatory information contradictory to the views of the president. This was just one of several sites contrived by Big Brother to supervise and scrutinize those opposed to Obama's policies. Back in 2012 the president's people launched a web site called, Attack Watch, which was designed to stop any smear verbiage about him or his office. The site goaded fellow Americans to rat out friends and neighbors who were preaching discord toward the president and his socialistic agenda. When many conservatives mocked the site, it was later removed and replaced with the subsequent, Truth Team. This more subtle approach to oversight was designed to debunk myths and lies about the president. The site still exists today.[29]

Does an honest man lie about his accreditations? On the campaign trail back in 2008, Obama frequently toted himself a former University of Chicago congressional law professor. The proclamation promoted the university to release a statement that year asserting that Obama was never accredited with title of Professor of Law. Mr. Obama was in fact a lecturer at the university between 1992 and 1996. A lecturer is not a full time profession. There is a big discrepancy between

---

[29] John MacHaffie, REPUBLIC NOW - Galactic News, September 17th, 2013.

119

instructor and professor. For one thing, an instructor lacks the appropriate credentials of a professor. In his first year at the university, Obama only taught one course. Several years later his course load grew to only three a semester— well short of a full course load required of a certified professor. In fact, Mr. Obama is no longer a lawyer. He surrendered his license to practice law back in 2008 amongst speculation that he lied on his bar application. Michelle Obama, back in 1993, "voluntarily surrendered" her license to practice law under suspicions of insurance fraud. A person doesn't usually "voluntarily surrender" their law license unless they were accused of gross misconduct. It's not like you lose your qualifications if you don't renew your license. Case in point, Bill Clinton voluntarily retired his law license after he admitted to lying in the Monica Lewinski cover-up.[30]

On August 27, 2012, Chris Matthews, the host of *Hardball* verbally castigated Republican National Committee Chairman, Reince Priebus on *MSNBC's*, *Morning Joe*. Matthews attacked Priebus, accusing Mitt

---

[30] Brenda Battle Jordan, "The Obama's, I Knew They Had Both Lost Their Law License, But I Didn't Know Why Until I Read This," Before It's News, Friday, March 1, 2013 15:54.

Romney of playing the "race card" after Romney made an Obama birth certificate joke at a campaign rally in Commerce, Michigan. Never once during the berating did Matthews condemn the Obama camp for implying Romney was a tax cheat. If Mr. Matthews continues pointing a disparaging finger, accusing people of being racists, then I think he should direct his hypocritical opinions toward our fearless leader. Does anyone hold this president accountable for condemning a greater number of blacks and Hispanics to poverty than any other politician in our history? It's funny how Matthews always attempts to draw attention towards race, but we Americans have a right to know where our president was born. If Obama's not a natural-born citizen of this country, he is immediately disqualified to be our president. According to Obama's own paternal grandmother, Sarah Onyango Obama, the president was born in Kenya. She also alleged that she was present at the delivery, giving validity to her claim. Grandmother Sarah's assertion is shared by the president's half-brother and half-sister.

The circumstances surrounding Obama's birth are convoluted at best. We still don't know exactly which hospital Obama was born, Kapiolani Hospital or Queens Hospital in

Honolulu.[31] Many critics claim that Obama's birth certificate, outlining that he was born in Hawaii, is a forgery. There are a number of inconsistencies on the birth certificate produced by the White House in 2008. Under nationality, the birth document lists Barak Obama Senior's race as African, but back in 1961 the modern usage of African or African American wasn't conceived. People of color were called Negros and documented as such.[32] The birth certificate also states that Obama's father, Barak Senior, was born in Kenya, East Africa. However, back in 1961 Kenya was a British colony called British East Africa Protectorate. The Republic of Kenya didn't exist until two years after Obama was born. Also, the certificate's listed hospital of birth, Kapiolani Maternity & Gynecological Hospital, didn't acquire its name until 1978. Back 1961, the hospital was called Kaui Keolani Children's Hospital and Kapi'olani Maternity Home.[33] Lastly, the birth

---

[31] Leo Berman, "The hospital listed on Barack Obama's just-publicized long-form birth certificate denies the president was born there," Texas Tribune, April 27th, 2011.

[32] Dr. Conspiracy, "The African Race," Obama Conspiracy Theories, April 3, 2009.

[33] Spencer Dahl, "Four Simple Questions," Bend Bugle, August 20, 2012.

certificate fails to mention the weight of the baby. A *CBS* broadcast from March 17, 2013 claims that Barak Obama's birth certificate is a forgery. The document was created via a computer program and generated using layers of existing birth certificates. The investigative team responsible for presenting this evidence indicated that if the digital copy was created by a scan, then layers wouldn't appear on only a single digital document.

Obama's own lawyer, Alexandra Hill, during a recent New Jersey ballot challenge, attested to the fact that the image of Obama's birth certificate was a forgery.[34]

Further fueling the debate of Obama's origins, Obama's book publicist listed in the president's bio that he was born in Kenya. Whether the accusation was correct or the inference was used to glamorize the president's genealogy, Obama never corrected the oversight. It wasn't until running for the Illinois State Senate seventeen years later that the biography was changed to read Mr. Obama was

---

[34] Penbrook Johannson, "Obama Lawyer Admits Forgery but disregards "image" as Indication of Obama's Ineligibility Damage Control," The Tea Party Tribune, Thursday, April 12, 2012.

born in Hawaii. In April of 2008, the Associated Press ran a story that President Obama's transcripts from Occidental College showed Obama received financial aid after claiming status as a foreign student from Indonesia. It's still unclear whether Obama actually received the fellowship after claiming Indonesian citizenship, but the fact remains the president spent millions of dollars to keep his records concealed from the American public. Obama sealed his college records from Occidental, Columbia and Harvard. If the president has nothing to hide, why not come clean? Often a guilty man shrouds suspicion of his innocence by hiding the truth.

An article in MrConservative.com dated May 15, 2013 lists the records sealed by the president:[35]

Original, long-form 1961 Hawaiian birth certificate.
Marriage license between Obama's father (Barak Sr.) and mother (Stanley Ann Dunham)

---

[35] Anonymous, "Alabama Supreme Court Reviews Shocking Evidence Obama's Birth Certificate Likely A Forgery," MrConservatice.com, May 15, 2013 7:06pm PST.

Name change (Barry Sotero to Barack Hussein Obama)

Obama's adoption records

Records of Obama's and his mother's repatriation as US citizens on return from Indonesia

Obama's baptism records

Noelani Elementary School (Hawaii)

Punahou School financial aid or school records

Occidental College financial aid records

Harvard Law School records

Columbia senior thesis

Columbia College records

Obama's record with Illinois State Bar Association

Obama's files from career as an Illinois State Senator

Obama's law client list

Obama's medical records

Obama's passport records

Chapter 10

Is Obama's Foreign policy a success?

Growing up in New York, I never had the privilege to serve in the United States Military. I do, however, have a profound appreciation and respect for our brave men and women who put themselves in harm's way on a daily basis. It is these brave individuals who protect our freedoms and the rights of all Americans. Our nation can never repay them for the debt they've endowed us. I was outraged during the presidential debates when President Obama claimed that our military petitioned for downsizing, calling for sequestration (sequestration is a mandatory cut in government spending). Logically, why would any member of the armed services consent to a program designed to potentially phase out their job and their ability to provide for their family? Likewise, why would any military employee agree to a program designed to weaken our capacity to defend ourselves and our global interests? American citizens must make a priority of helping the people that selflessly guard our security and the American way of life.

Downsizing our armed services by possibly 50% over the next eight years would cripple the readiness and modernization of our military forces. Sequestration would cut $1.3 trillion out of the defense budget over the ensuing decade, potentially eliminating one million private sector and government held jobs. Many forecast that the maneuver would decimate our military, leaving our country with the smallest armed forces since World War I. Not only does the plan call for drastic downsizing of our military personnel, but mandates spending cuts across the board for other essential programs and equipment. Besides the numerous military installations on the chopping block designated for closure, the Marines and Army could lose fifteen ground divisions. The navy could non-commission over three hundred ships and the air force could lose almost two-thousand aircraft. In my opinion, sequestration is a crime that weakens our ability to defend ourselves at home and abroad. In fact, military spending seems the only part of the federal budget that Obama is willing to negotiate on and cut to reduce our annual deficit.

Why not just halt foreign aid to the radical extremist and middle-eastern nations who scorn us and redirect the funds to our veterans? Why pay almost six billion in government aid earmarked each year to countries like Egypt, Afghanistan and Pakistan and rededicate these resources to preserving our military? Why continue hurting the people we love while supporting and funding those who hate us? In my opinion, this is not only bad policy, but the very principle is downright immoral. The Obama administration recently denied $100,000 "death gratuity" to the families of soldiers killed in the line of duty. In a shrewd maneuver the Defense Department redefined the interpretation of the law for granting these provisional gratuities, which disqualified death benefits for many of the families of our fallen heroes. According to a recent article in The Last Refuge, "President Obama's administration *interpreted* the congressional Pay Our Military Act to exclude payments of the Death Gratuity."[36]

Under the sequestration provisions, the administration is slashing pay increases and health benefits for active military personnel while dramatically increasing healthcare costs to our veterans. By hacking away at our defense budget to the tune of $1.3 trillion over the next eight years the move will decimate our

---

[36] Sundance, "Spite House" – President Stompy Feet Rules Now Deny Military Active Duty Combat "Death Gratuity" Benefit….," The Last Refuge, October 9, 2013.

military and jeopardize our national security home and abroad. Not only will it decrease the quantity and caliber of our international presence, but it will drastically reduce our covert Intelligence necessary to stem the cultivation of radical Islamic terrorist groups. Sequestration will mean cuts to essential military training programs. Leaving our soldiers unprepared to operate in the field will only serve to unnecessarily place their lives in danger. Not only is our federal government attempting to make the lives of our military personnel more difficult, but sequestration may ultimately dissuade others from joining the armed services. During the recent government shut down, there were claims that the administration used our veterans as pawns to gain political leverage over the republicans. The G.O.P. asserted that the White House was attempting to make the government shutdown as "painful for the American people as possible." The administration closed national parks. They also shut down war monuments, threatening litigation to any attempting to bypass the blockades that were fortifying these monuments. Expressing their disdain, the idle threats didn't stop thousands of protestors and veterans from breaching the barricades at the World War II memorial. Lending credence to our leader's deceitful ploy was the fact that it cost more to barricade and arm the monuments than it did to keep them open. The famed Ford Theatre where Lincoln was shot was also temporarily closed due to the shut down even though no federal employee works at the theatre, it's a non-profit organization and NO federal funds are used to maintain operations there. When Governor Chris Christie was pegged in a supposed scandal involving the intentional shut down of lanes on the George Washington Bridge to increase the discomfort in our lives the mainstream media continues to call for his lynching. However, when Obama shuts down our national parks and war monuments to also increase our stress-levels the media hypocritically overlooks the same devious strategy.

It's appalling that our government treats our military personnel so disrespectfully, that the White House uses every insidious tactical ploy to undermine the welfare of our veterans, yet if you serve one term in Congress you're guaranteed a lifelong pension. Does anyone see the irony in the fact that our veterans can't get a fair shake under this president, but an ex-congressional leader like Jesse Jackson Jr., currently serving a thirty year prison sentence after pleading guilty to the misappropriation of

$750,000 in campaign contributions, may still be eligible to receive his lifetime pension after paroled? What kind of world are we living in?

Back in 2012, Israel Prime minister, Benjamin Netanyahu, petitioned an immediate conference with our president to discuss the developing Iranian nuclear crisis. He travelled to New York to specifically meet with Obama. However, it was more important for our fearless leader to appear on Letterman to promote his reelection chances. The White House at the time claimed that no such counsel was petitioned and that's why the two leaders failed to hold a conference. Even if this ridiculous assertion by the White House is valid, isn't it the responsibility of the United States President, the leader of the "free world", to demand an immediate audience with the Israeli Prime Minister over the impending threat? Don't we as a nation have a commitment to defend the sovereignty of our greatest Middle Eastern ally or at the very least protect the American people? At the time, then Iranian President, Mahmoud Ahmadinejad, expressed a desire to destroy Israel and "eliminate the Zionist regime." Many would argue that Israeli foreign affairs is of no concern of ours, but this is naive thinking. Iran is the world's leading state supporter of terrorism. If Iran is able to go uncontested with regards to developing their nuclear program, what makes you think that the Iranians wouldn't trade this knowledge off to terrorist groups like Hezbollah, Al-Qaida, and Hamas? What do you think will happen if Al-Qaida gets there hands on a dirty bomb? Can you say bye-bye New York, boys and girls?

Further empowering our enemies, our international military capabilities were severely fractured when, back in 2009, Obama discarded our missile defense programs in Poland and The Czech Republic. We essentially reneged on our commitment to these two nations, which made us look weak in the eyes of our enemies and forsaken in the eyes of our allies throughout the world. Outlined in an article by James Carafano of *The Foundry*, the Russians rejected Obama's offers to abandon the construction of our missile defense system in Europe in return for dissuading the Iran government to abandon their nuclear program.

"The Russians have already said "No!" to this. And with good reason…they are selling nuclear technology and air defenses to protect nuclear sites to the Iranians. Even if the Russians said "Yes" the Iranians would say "No." They have no interest in giving up their weapons program as a favor to the Russians. And even if the Iranians said "Yes" it would take years to negotiate a verification system to prove they really were disarming…and in that time could covertly build missiles and nuclear weapons…and if we stopped building missile defenses now we would be caught with no defense."[37]

Why the hell are we diminishing our military capability around the globe when we aren't getting anything in return for our efforts? The superfluous move only serves to weaken our ability to defend ourselves from future attacks around the globe. This is a massive failure on the part of our president to protect our national interests and the botched measure most likely expedited the Iran Nuclear Program. Obama also failed to support the Iranian democracy uprising in 2009, allowing the Islamic Fundamentalist to remain in power. To show his continued commitment to Islamic Fundamentalist on the wake of the Benghazi Tragedy, Obama spoke at the United Nations. Still blaming the attack on our consulate on the anti-Islamic video he said, *"The future must not belong to those who slander The Prophet of Islam."* How can our government run an effective foreign policy when our president

---

[37] James Carafano, "Missile Mayhem," The Foundry, March 4, 2009 at 9:37 am.

missed over 60% of his intelligence briefings?

Under Obama's foreign policy, our enemies no longer fear us and our allies no longer trust us. Obama caters to the leaders of Middle-Eastern countries and foreign dictators. He bowed before the King of Saudi Arabia, Chinese President Hu Jintao and the Emperor of Japan.

According to a recent *Washington Times* article: "President Obama has disgraced the United States—again. During this week's nuclear summit in Washington, he bowed when greeting Chinese President Hu Jintao. The act was not only shocking but revealing. Mr. Obama has come under intense criticism for bowing to leaders in the past—the king of Saudi Arabia, the emperor of Japan. But never before has America's commander in chief prostrated himself to a foreign tyrant on US soil. By bowing, Mr. Obama degraded and cheapened the office of the presidency; as Commander in Chief, he represents every American when meeting with other heads of state. He is supposed to embody the dignity of the Oval Office, reflecting our collective heritage as a self-governing, constitutional republic."[38]

Outlined in a recent article in *MotherJones*, the US prestige and influence in the Middle East is in a "death spiral." No one there respects us or fears us.[39] The radical Islamic elements in these countries witness the faltering US economy and realize that our abilities to support an imperialistic presence there is unrealistic. All they need to do is wait us out. Obama provides clear and precise timelines for evacuating our troops, which enhances our enemies' knowledge of our intentions and causes trepidation in the minds of our allies. If someone told me that they were pulling out on a Monday, I'd stockpile my armaments for a raid on Tuesday— it's not rocket science. The non-radical Fundamentalist in the Middle East already hate us due to the Afghani and Iraqi wars and are unwilling to provide intelligence and support. Our allies dispersed when we threatened to strike Syria and the Assad regime after Syria used chemical

---

[38] Jeffrey T. Kuhner, "KUHNER: Obama bowing to the world," The Washington Times, Friday, April 16, 2010.

[39] Robert Dreyfuss, "How American Foreign Policy Is Hurting American Power," MotherJones.com, Tues Nov. 5, 2013 11:13 AM PST.

weapons on its own people. This European dissent demonstrated that our friends around the world neither trust us nor support our global initiatives. When Obama sought the abdication of Assad, the Syrian leader solicited and was granted refuge by Russia and Iran. The move was an embarrassment to our country and showed how impotent and ineffectual our international leadership has become. When Obama petitioned Congress for the direct use of military force in Syria, our congressional leaders rejected the initiative. This was in direct contrast to ten years prior when Congress overwhelmingly endorsed Bush's retaliation on Iraq. How did the Iraqis repay us for effectuating their independence—they "bitch-slapped" Obama by refusing any US military presence whatsoever in Iraq after the war ended.

We've alienated our two largest allies in the Middle East. Israel and Saudi Arabia no longer trust us after our government backed Mohamed Morsi and Egypt's Muslim Brotherhood by giving the radical extremists $1.5 billion each year in foreign aid. We provide mixed signals to the Saudis by failing to take serious initiatives to deter Iran's nuclear program and failing to act against Syria's use of chemical weapons by our refusal to oust Syrian president Assad from power. Our commitment to sequestration could possibly mean the closure of many US military bases in the Middle East, which are currently a security comfort to abounding Egyptians. The move leaves Egyptian sovereignty questioning whether we still "have their back." Meanwhile, we've placed Israel in a precarious situation. Our unwillingness to take the Iran nuclear crisis seriously and force the Iranians to abandon their nuclear program forces the Israeli prime minister to consider a solitary pre-empted strike against Iran before Iran develops the capability to enrich uranium. According to a Reuters report: "Upset at President Barack Obama's policies on Iran and Syria, members of Saudi Arabia's ruling family are threatening a rift with the United States that could take the alliance between Washington and the kingdom to its lowest point in years."[40]

---

[40] Amena Bakr and Warren Strobel, "Saudi Arabia warns of shift away from U.S. over Syria, Iran," Reuters, Tue Oct. 22, 2013 8:27pm EDT.

"I am in no mood to be deceived any longer by the crafty devil and false character whose greatest pleasure is to take advantage of everyone."

- Camille Claudel

Chapter 11

How is our debt hurting us?

When President Obama appeared on David Letterman back in September, 2012, Letterman asked Obama if our overwhelming debt is hurting our economy. President Obama responded, "That our debt may hurt us in the future but it isn't something we have to worry about today." Here is a president either blatantly lying to the American people about the severity of our debt crisis or he is blissfully ignorant to the ramifications of our dire fiscal situation. We are currently on pace to double our national debt under this president. This statistical anomaly means that President Obama has effectively accumulated more debt than all other presidents combined. In his five years in office, Mr. Obama has managed to increase our expenditures at the same amplitude as our previous 230 year history collectively.

According to a recent somber article published by *PressTV* the drastic explosion of our national debt is reaching alarming proportions. In today's market we enjoy the luxury of a 2% interest rate. If this rate climbs back to 6% (the interest rate ten years ago), the added burden will essentially collapse the US economy. As a matter of fact, our government debt rose over 60% in the last five years alone while GDP grew at a nominal rate of less than 9%. This means that the National Debt to GDP ratio increased from 65% to over 100% since Obama took office. To put things in perspective, our debt is currently at the point where every man woman and child in this country individually owe over fifty thousand dollars to pay off our national debt. We've mortgaged our children's and grandchildren's future to the point that they owe one hundred million dollars each day on our current loans and more than a third of these loans are to international creditors. Our fiscal obligations currently exceed a third of the world's entire debt. To give you a perspective on how much we owe, if you spend a million dollars every single hour of every single day since the birth of Jesus Christ (factoring in interest) we still wouldn't pay back our loans. In fact, it's common knowledge that our entitlement programs are currently increasing six times faster than our population growth. In the following years our Social Security system is expected a shortfall, exceeding $175 trillion over the next seventy-five years and under Obamacare, sixteen million new Medicaid participants are expected to enroll into the program. The explosion of Medicaid inductees will decimate our already fragile economy.[41]

Washington and the President are recklessly spending money we don't have and seem content with destroying our great nation. The oversight is compromising our children's future. The lapdog liberal media are zealously complacent on disregarding our "runaway spending", defending a corrupt president who is **intentionally** leading us down a destructive path. They refuse to report the dismal picture of our floundering economy and the catastrophic ramifications on spending as it equates to our destined bleak future. They refuse to acknowledge that our spending will inevitably lead to a collapse of the American dollar. It's not a matter of "if this will happen," but rather "when it will happen." We are borrowing so much money that soon we can't print enough to repay even the interest on our loans. The American people either don't seem to care about our uncontrollable spending or are

---

[41] HJ, "33 stats national debt is destroying America," PressTV, Sat Oct 19, 2013 1:15PM GMT.

ignorant to this encroaching derailment of the US economy. The republicans and Tea Party delegates are ostracized in the media for attempting to pull back the reins of uncontrollable spending and seem helpless in defending themselves and the American people against the persistent bullying of Nancy Pelosi, Harry Reid, and the executive branch.

Right now the only thing keeping the American economy solvent is the US dollar. Since oil is priced in US dollars, Americans benefit from a proprietary contingency due to the positioning of our currency. The US Dollar is the world's reserve currency and embodies the world's financial structure. It's the currency that the central banks around the globe hold in reserve as currency against their loans. Due to this unique relationship, Americans benefit from discounted pricing on international imports. If Germany wants to buy oil from OPEC, they're required to purchase it in US dollars. This is why most Asian and European countries pay nearly three times the cost for a gallon of gasoline then we pay here in the States. The Fed can continue to print $75 billion dollars each month to keep our debt in check without experiencing the typical effects of inflation and hyperinflation due to the devaluation of our currency, because it's the world's economy that is currently assuming the impact of the detrimental costs of our irresponsible spending by furnishing our government with enormous loans. These loans are strangling the US economy as well as many economies throughout the world. The fact that the US dollar is the world's monetary reserve protects us (at least for the time being) from economic turmoil. It's our proprietary status that prevents our economy from collapsing and turning out like the obliterated economies of Greece and Spain. In the last several years alone the US dollar has devalued by 12%.

Long-term debt will hurt our country's future growth. As a hypothetical example, fifteen years ago I bought that state-of-the-art 32-inch Sony cathode-tube television. It was awesome at the time. I used my MasterCard to pay for the expensive purchase, but in the fifteen years I owned the television, I only paid off the interest on the credit-card bill and never paid down the principal. Recently I was eying that new Sony L.E.D. high-definition flat-screen television at Best Buy, but since I haven't paid off my credit card bill from the last expenditure, I can't afford this new technology. Now I'm stuck with that obsolete clunker. The preceding example is a basic model of how debt hinders progress, but in reality, our enormous debt will eventually affect our country's ability to develop new technology, support higher-education, erect new construction, and facilitate programs geared at maintaining our country's infrastructure.

If you think we can't lose our premier status in the world, look what happened to the British economy after their currency collapsed in the 1970s. Following WWII, through the Marshall Plan, the United States bailed out Britain and other European countries whose economies were shattered by the war. For more than one hundred and fifty years the British Sterling was the world's reserve currency. When Britain shifted towards a socialistic agenda back in the early 1970s, their economy quickly spiraled downward. Similar to President Obama, Britain's Labour Party wanted to "spread the wealth." After taking over the country's major industries and intentionally devaluing their currency to cap inflation, their economy was upended almost overnight.

Since our federal government is the only entity permitted to print currency and our states are not, our provinces are raising taxes and selling off assets to balance their overwhelming deficits. Thirty-three states reported shortfalls last year. Some state economies like California are in serious trouble, and in 2013, the city of Detroit was the largest municipal bankruptcy filing in the history of the United States. Sixty years of liberal leadership, big unions and corruption decimated the city. Once a thriving metropolis of 1.8 million residents, the municipality is today a fragmented shell of its former self. Only 700,000 residents remain in a town that once boasted the highest income per capita in the country. This is a 75% decline in population over the last decade and of the 25% remaining, 60% of the city's children currently live in poverty. This once thriving city is now ravished with destitution, crime and gang-related violence. Back in 2011, the crime rate in Detroit rose a whopping 78% that year.

According to a 2013 article published in The Economic Collapse, "Cities such as Detroit, Chicago, Milwaukee, Cleveland, Philadelphia and Baltimore were all teeming with economic activity and the rest of the globe looked on our economic miracle with a mixture of wonder and envy. But now look at us. Our once proud cities are being transformed into poverty-stricken hellholes. Sadly, the exact same thing that is happening to Detroit is happening to cities all over America. Detroit is just ahead of the curve. We are in the midst of a long-term economic collapse that is eating away at us like cancer, and things are going to get a lot worse than this. So if you still live in a prosperous area of the country, don't laugh at what is happening to others. What is happening to them will be coming to your area soon enough."[42]

Most American's don't understand the repercussions of losing our status as the world's currency reserve. As other countries around the world begin to lose faith in the US dollar, interest rates will skyrocket, because countries like China will begin tightening up on credit, and foreign investors will look to diversify risk by investing in other forms of currency like gold and silver. Is it any wonder that the price of precious metals has gone through the roof in recent years? This move will in turn force the Federal Reserve to print more money to pay back our overwhelming debt. When there are boatloads of US dollars floating around the globe, our currency devalues as demand for the dollar diminishes. The move will result in extraordinary inflation for America. The costs of foreign imports like produce from South America, electronics from China and cars from Germany and Japan will soar overnight, forcing

---

[42] Michael Snyder, "America the Fallen: 24 Signs That Our Once Proud Cities Are Turning Into Poverty-Stricken Hellholes," The Economic Collapse, April 23rd, 2013.

Americans to buy only American goods and services. The costs of commodities in this country will also increase as gasoline prices spike. Trucking companies, forced to incur higher overhead due to the escalated fuel costs, will pass down the costs, increasing delivery expenses to the manufacturing companies. These manufacturing companies will in turn raise their costs to the consumer to maintain any form of profitability. Since the United States is the largest consumer in the world, the price of manufactured goods from other countries will decrease as demand decreases. Many European countries will scramble to unload their heavily-discounted products in the global marketplace. This desperate move will result in a drastic hit to the economies of many foreign countries. If the US dollar collapses, financial institutions in this country could go bankrupt overnight, wiping out the savings of millions of Americans. The stock market could crash instantaneously. Some may argue that "who cares if we owe money, that won't hurt us today," but we are currently experiencing a massive decline in our economy that matches that of The Great Depression. At this rate, our nation is on an unsustainable and inevitable path towards destruction!

According to an article this year by *Business Insider*, the Chinese are actively taking measures to wean themselves off the US dollar. They are extremely concerned with the United States Government's mishandling of our currency. They are attempting to implement cross-border regulations with their own currency (the Yuan) and other European and Asian currencies. The incorporation of an international monetary policy would diversify the risk of a single world reserve currency and will ultimately have an abysmal weakening effect on the US economy. It may take years for this transition to occur, but it the United States fails to either decrease spending, or continues to irresponsibly increase the debt ceiling by borrowing more money, we could default on our loans. The disastrous move would probably expedite the need for a change towards an international monetary policy. The predicament would leave the United States in a profoundly weakened position.

"China is actively taking steps to phase out the US dollar which will decrease volatility in oil and commodity prices and deride the 'exorbitant privilege' the USA commands as the issuer of the reserve currency at the centre of a post-war international financial architecture which is now failing."[43]

---

[43] Goldcore Bullion and Wealth Management Company, "China Wants to Wean Itself off The Dollar, But Risks

Another way China is trying to take over as the world's number one economy is through oil. Traditionally oil is priced in US dollars. China continues snubbing their noses in the American's faces by remaining the largest importer of oil from Iran even though the world leaders sanctioned Iran due to the escalating nuclear threat. China is reselling massive amounts of this oil on the global exchange to subvert America's control over the oil market

Don't fool yourselves, there is a global economic war currently transpiring and it's coming to a theatre near you. China and Russia are salivating at the chance to push America over the fiscal cliff and take over as the world's leading economy. China has warned that if the US eventually defaults on their loans, China may decide to stop buying American dollars altogether. The move would have catastrophic consequences to the US economy. China's leading news agency, Xinhua, in a recent column, harshly criticized America's fiscal irresponsibility. The Op-ed read: "The "pernicious impasse" warrants a move to a "de-Americanized world." The article further went on to state, "The cyclical stagnation in

---

Destroying Chinese Wealth," Business Insider, Jan. 22, 2013, 6:12 PM

Washington for a viable bipartisan solution over a federal budget and an approval for raising debt ceiling has again left many nations' tremendous dollar assets in jeopardy and the international community highly agonized."[44]

Even though the Chinese are the largest producers of gold in the world, for the last several years they've been importing and hording massive amounts of gold in an attempt to back the Yuan in gold. The move is significant because it allows China to not depend solely on a US currency, which stunts the growth of its own economy. China is also looking to diversify their risks by weaning off US Treasury Bonds and redirect investments in European and Asian real estate. Recently, China has made back-door currency-swap agreements with England and other European nations. The move is significant because it gives global credibility to the Yuan and to China's advances towards internationalizing their currency. China is attempting to place a great deal of pressure on the global stage to switch to a world reserve currency. They're pushing for this move by 2015.

[44]Charles Riley, "World chastises U.S. as debt ceiling looms," CNN Money, October 14, 2013: 12:42 PM ET

Make no mistake that China has become very crafty on their method of undermining the world's confidence in the US currency and we're giving them ample ammunition to take us down. If we fail to grow up and figure out a way to control our runaway spending then it's only a matter of time before other European, Asian and South American countries follow China's lead and attempt to ditch the US dollar for a more financially stable and powerful world currency. Many countries are upset with the United States and blame us for depressing many of their own economies. They are desperate and quickly tiring of America's reckless borrowing. Just remember that when you trap a rat in a corner, that rat will bite.

"Our liberty cannot be guarded but by the freedom of the press, nor that be limited without danger of losing it."

- Thomas Jefferson to John Jay, 1786.

Chapter 12

How is the mainstream liberal media aiding in the destruction of America?

The "conventional" media has become an industry focused on maximizing their revenues and market shares. Like all other businesses, these large news distribution channels are geared towards making a profit. They are subject to media-bias, because they attempt to appease their target audience. Instead of reporting the news objectively, these media outlets tend to report information geared towards the reader's political point of view or their political interests. The reason why news organizations like MSNBC, CBS, The New York Times, The Washing Post and The L.A. Times refuse to report the radical agenda of our president or how his policies are harming America, is because the majority populations of our major cities consist of democrats. Not only is the demography of our major cities heavily populated towards this political affiliation, but many of the states maintaining the most electoral votes are heavily democratic. These demographics are especially true of, New York, California, Pennsylvania, Ohio, Illinois and Connecticut. Artist, William G. Ballester once said, *"Give the people what they want, and they will give you what you want."*

The liberal media helps promote Obama's radical agenda by continuing to bash the conservatives and promote progressive liberalism. It's a given fact that readers and viewers exposed constantly to slanted far-left liberal ideologies will increase their probability of adopting liberal views. Nowadays, the mainstream media fail to report the "truth." Founding Fathers, Thomas Jefferson and Benjamin Franklin were staunch proponents of the "Freedom of the Press." They felt that it is the responsibility of the press to seek the truth and report it unfettered. For all of his philanthropy, his major contributions to our country's fabrication and all of his inventions, Franklin considered himself a newspaper editor and printer first and foremost. Likewise, Jefferson realized that the press was the great equalizing medium, keeping the general populace informed about the workings of their government. It also holds the government in check from exploiting the needs and the rights of American citizens.

In many oppressed cultures and communist societies, the main method these governments use to control the masses is by managing the information flowing to the general populace. The way they do this is by controlling the media. Hitler and Goebbels where staunch proponents of dominating their people through the use of propaganda. They were very effective in promoting German idealism and convincing their people to abandon and give up their fellow countryman. They condoned and justified the Holocaust. Hitler equated the mass extermination of the Jews with the very survival and prosperity of Germany and the German people bought into the pretense. Lenin and Stalin used the media to promote their socialistic agenda. Recently, North Korea, in an extreme show of censorship, executed eighty of its citizens. The reasoning behind the mass execution was prompted because the accused either possessed a Bible or watched a South Korean movie. In the end these liberal media sources will only serve to undermine their own credibility by failing to report the truth. A credibility issue isn't something you can recover from easily. We now see that the American people are developing a thirst for the "truth." A greater number of people are abandoning the mainstream media for secondary news outlets, like, talk radio, the internet, blogs and chat rooms.

The mainstream liberal news did this country a great disservice after they vetted presidential candidate Barack Obama back in 2008 when he first burst onto the national scene. Virtually unproven in the political arena, Obama's qualifications in handling the country's most important position were gratuitous at best. The media's dereliction of duty for failing to do their jobs and question Obama's competency to hold the office crippled our nation's ability to make a prudent decision during the time of the election. Besides failing to report the obvious Obama scandals like Benghazi, Fast and Furious, the NSA snooping on Americans, and the IRS targeting conservative groups, they never questioned back in 2008 what Obama meant by his promise to "Fundamentally change America." They never investigated Obama's ties with radical elements like University of Chicago professor Bill Ayers. Ayers is the former leader of the "Weather Underground," a radical left-wing organization dedicated to overthrowing the US government via violent revolution. The media never pressed Obama on his relationship with Reverend Jeremiah Wright. Wright was Obama's pastor for many years. An extremist, Pastor Wright sermonized often denouncing the United States of America and accusing our government of *"crimes against people of color."*[45] He also said in a speech, *"God damn America"* for its racism and *"for killing innocent people."*[46] The press never questioned Obama when "he was caught on a "hot mike" promising the President of Russia that he would cave in to their demands for a weaker missile shield—after he was re-elected and no longer had to keep up the pretense that he sought to defend America."[47]

The mainstream press never reported or explored Obama's incredulous relationship with Frank Marshall Davis, a member of the US Communist Party. Marshall was a mentor and important influence on shaping the social ideologies of a young and impressionable

---

[45] Brian Ross, "Obama's Pastor: God Damn America, U.S. to Blame for 9/11," ABC News, Retrieved 2008-03-17.

[46] Charles Babington (Associated Press), "Analysis: Obama grabs race issue," Yahoo! News, Retrieved 2008-03-18.

[47] John MacHaffie, "The Complete List of Barack Obama's Scandals, Misdeeds, Crimes and Blunders," REPUBLIC NOW - Galactic News, September 17th, 2013.

future president. They never reported Obama's ties to ACORN—an anti-capitalist group or that his brother is a self-proclaimed socialist. They never investigated Obama senior's support for socialist policies. Barack Obama senior published an academic paper back in 1965 entitled *Problems Facing Our Socialism,* advising then Kenyan President, Jomo Kenyatta, on how to fix the faltering Kenyan economy. The paper discouraged the president from, "relying on private investors, private capital, and private property ownership, as a means of improving the country's dreadful economy." Instead, "Mr. Obama proposed higher taxes on the wealthy, and a redistribution of that money, for the "collective good" of the nation."[48]

The liberal media refuse to acknowledge the pervasive pattern of Obama's lies, scandals and deceits. In the greatest cover-up in our nation's history, the main-stream media refuse to address the dire issues surrounding the destruction of our economy. They refuse to report the corruption and billions of taxpayer dollars wasted through cap

---

[48] Austin Hill, "The American Dream, or the Dreams of Obama's Father?" Townhall.com, Aug 19, 2012.

and trade. They failed to communicate the detrimental effects of the stimulus package and the fact that Obamacare will not only destroy our economy, but will redefine our constitution and America as we know it.

"The consequences of the mainstream media not doing their job are many and significant. Since failing to do their job we have elected the most radical president in the nation's history. This has allowed government officials, including President Obama, to place other radicals throughout our government including policy making positions that can create or cause long term structural problems for the government and the nation generally. We have seen the quadrupling of the nation's debt in one year which has resulted in the threatened downgrading of our credit rating for the first time in our history. We have seen a significant rise in the division of classes, between the poor, rich and middle class that has resulted in a level of envy, distrust and frustration unanticipated by Americans when we elected Obama. We have seen a government take-over of industries unlike anything that has occurred in the past. This includes the automotive industry, banks, education, and health care and now we see efforts directed towards energy. We have seen the demonetization of groups and organizations to further divide Americans in order for the administration to further its goals. Tea Party participants are called radicals, racists, and bigots simply for demanding that our government operate within the confines of the Constitution. We have seen our president bow and extend a hand of friendship to dictators and enemies of America while shunning and brow beating our allies and friends. We have seen the greatest number of radicals, communist and Marxist placed in high government positions and who now advocate policies and programs that will fit the framework of transforming America into a European styled socialist democracy. By refusing to ask "why" the liberal media is helping to destroy America as we know and love it. They have elected to join with this arrogant administration to dismiss and dismantle an enormously successful, over 200 year-old experiment that created the greatest nation ever and replace it with what they perceive to be a better governing system"[49]

---

[49] BQL Editor, "How the Liberal Media is Destroying America," Blackquillandink.com, October 25th, 2010.

"We are the music makers, and we are the dreamers of dreams."

- Arthur O'Shaughnessy.

Chapter 13

Is the United States still the greatest country on the face of the planet?

During a 2012 episode of the HBO series, Newsroom actor, Jeff Daniels was asked by a member of a studio audience "Why America is still the greatest country?" While the rest of the panel pandered to the audience talking about American "exceptionalism," Daniels delivered a disturbing and honest monologue on why the United States is no longer number one. He spouted off a plethora of statistical data to support his claim. He said that the United States is ranked seventh in literacy, twenty-seventh in math, twenty-second in science, forty-ninth in life expectancy, third in median household income and fourth in exports. Mr. Daniels went on to further explain that the United States only leads the world in several categories; the number of incarcerated cluttering our prisons and our inflated defense spending. Turning somber, Daniel's explained, we were the greatest country, but not anymore. "We once stood up to injustice and promoted decency. We sacrificed and cared about our neighbors. We built great things and made great amazing technological advances. We produced the world's greatest artists and developed the world's greatest economy. We didn't belittle intelligence, we inspired for the stars." He ended his soliloquy by stating that, *"The first step in solving a problem is admitting there is one."*

Are we still the greatest country in the world today? The answer is unequivocally, yes! What the statistical data fails to take into account is America's entrepreneurial spirit and drive to succeed. We are a diverse melting-pot of unbound ingenuity. Due largely to America's technological advances, the world has developed more in the last hundred years than the previous five billion years. The United States is greatly responsible for paving the way for the Industrial Revolution. We are the leaders in innovation and creative thinking. We are an amalgamation of exceptional scholars and risk takers. Our students may not have the highest test scores, but we are best at achieving greatness and imbuing this success. We are free and entrepreneurial thinkers who've produced some of the greatest artists and musicians. We innovate, we create, we inspire. We continually push the bounds of possibility and redefine the status quo. We don't ask "what or why?" we ask "what if or why not?" We take dreams and make them a reality. As a culture we may not rank amongst the highest test scores around the globe, but if we didn't have the best education system in the world, then why do all other nations send their promising students to learn in our institutions? The reason is because others want what we have. They want their respective countries to be as rich and as exceptional as the United States. This is why China sends over 200,000 of their students to learn in the United States each year.

As a nation we've made astounding advances in bio-science and space exploration. Great American physicists like Richard Feynman, Julian Schwinger and Albert Einstein redefined and expanded our knowledge of the universe. We cured diseases. Through extraordinary medical breakthroughs, we've increased the life expectancy of the world's population. Today 70% of all children afflicted with cancer beat the disease due to medical advancements developed here in the United States. We also pioneered modern medicine by inventing life-saving procedures like angioplasty and the catheter-delivered stent to help those suffering from heart disease. We developed the artificial heart, the pacemaker and the defibrillator, which save countless lives. Through the private sector our pharmaceutical companies have produced life-saving and life-altering medicines to help combat an entire host of ailments like high blood pressure, diabetes and high cholesterol. We have the best hospitals and even though our healthcare is expensive, we have the best doctors. We've developed vaccines to cure polio, chickenpox and smallpox. American inventor, Selman Abraham Waksman, invented several antibiotic medications to combat bacterial infections. It's the private sector that's responsible for our great advancements in biomedical research and our numerous medical achievements. The National Institute of Health is a prime example of how privatizing the medical industry can lead to ground-breaking strives in biomedicine and medical research.

Many have pondered why the United States was able to develop into the greatest economy and the greatest country the world has ever known. According to Wikipedia, the reason why America is so great is because, "The United States Constitution itself reflects the desire to encourage scientific creativity." It gives the United States Congress the power "to promote the progress of science and useful arts, by securing for limited times to authors and inventors the exclusive right to their respective writings and discoveries." This clause formed the basis for the U.S. patent and copyright systems, whereby creators of original art and technology would get a government granted monopoly, which after a limited period would become free to all citizens, thereby enriching the public domain."[50] So, it's not socialism that made America "the great land of opportunity." The reason we have the oldest government and the most successful economy is due to democracy, capitalism and free-enterprise. In a "free society" the individual is inspired to reach boundless limits.

When President Obama tells the American people that *"we didn't build that"*, his comments couldn't be farther from the truth. We invented, created and built more than any other nation that ever existed on this planet, period! We generated more wealth and more prosperity than any other country because of great thinkers like Henry Ford, Alexander Graham Bell, Jonas Salk, Nikola Tesla, Albert Einstein, the Wright Brothers, and Benjamin Franklin. We redefined modes of

---

[50] Science and technology in the United States, Wikipedia, http://en.wikipedia.org/wiki/Science_and_technology_in_the_United_States

transportation. We built the first automobile and the first airplane. We invented the locomotive and were the first to use trucking to transport our goods. We led the way in space-travel by creating the first manned spacecraft. America was the first to send a man to the moon after we developed the first rocket propulsion system. We've expanded our planet's knowledge of the universe by advancements in physics and space exploration to Mars and Saturn. We've created avenues of sharing ideas and information with the world through advancements in communications. We invented the personal computer, the communication satellite, the cell phone, the internet, the microchip, the transistor and social media outlets like Facebook and Twitter. We pioneered the way for keeping the world energy self-sufficient by developing advancements in renewable energy like wind, clean coal, solar and hydropower.

According to Wikipedia here is just a partial list of the great contributions American endowed the world: The hearing aid, the microphone, the telephone, the light bulb, electricity through the use of lightening, the transistor radio, the microwave oven, electrically-cooled refrigeration, Freon, the credit card (not sure this is a good thing), crash test dummies (no... not Obama, Pelosi or

Reid), the Cotton Gin, the suspension bridge, gaming consoles, Morse Code, crackers, the hamburger (yes, you guessed it, we also invented the cheeseburger), the potato chip, baseball, American football, blue jeans, escalators, passenger elevators, the sewing machine, the lathe, cereal, the circuit breaker, the skyscraper, the paper bag, the web printing press, the clothes hanger, the cash register, the can opener, the thermostat, the ball-point pen, the fly swatter, digital cameras, the phonograph, compact discs, the smoke detector, the tea bag, thumb tacks, the muffler, the machine gun, the tractor, nickel-cadmium batteries, the airbrush, power tools, the Ferris Wheel, the mousetrap, the assembly line, air conditioning, the hay baler, windshield wipers, remote control, ac power plugs and sockets, car transmissions, paper towels, curtain rods, the washing machine and dryer, the candy apple, headsets, the electric blanket, traffic cones, supermarkets, the light switch, torque wrenches, hydraulic breaks, the polygraph machine, garage doors, adhesive bandages, water skiing, cotton swabs, bulldozers, deodorant (you're welcome, France), masking tape, fiberglass, power steering, the electric razor, bubble gum, sunglasses, the car radio, the electric guitar (and electric bass), chocolate chip cookies, the golf cart, the parking meter, the trampoline, stock-car racing, the Philips head screwdriver, digital computers, nylon, the chainsaw, the bazooka, disposable diapers, supersonic aircraft, acrylic paint, the hairdryer and hand dryer, hairspray and the aerosol can, cable television, kitty litter, radioactive carbon dating, felt-tip pens, leaf blowers, coolers, the sliding door, nuclear submarines, video tape, the hard disk drive, WD-40, the integrated circuit board, Elvis and Frank Sinatra, motion pictures, wet suits, bar codes, Spandex, artificial turf, carbonated beverages, the laser diode, buffalo wings, John Wayne, snowboarding, microprocessors, the laser printer, Taser, the mouse pad, GPS, Gore-Tex, Popcorn bags, the space shuttle, Java script, paintball, bifocals, spray guns, the coffee pot, the revolver, the argon laser, the cordless telephone, the Heimlich Maneuver, firewalls, the burglar alarm, roller skates, LCD projection, oil refineries, the steamboat, the telegraph machine, Styrofoam, etc., and to-be-continued. As a matter of fact, America has invented and inspired so much that exactly one-half of all Nobel prizes awarded for the first half of the twentieth century were given to American lariats.

American exceptionalism means that we don't bow before the world; the world should thank their lucky stars for what the Americans brings to the table. The world benefits greatly from a prosperous and healthy United States. We are The United Nations, we are NATO, we are the International Space Station, and we are the world's financial center. We are the protector of the weak and defenseless. Hands down, we've provided more humanitarian aid than any country that ever existed. We've given billions of dollars in humanitarian relief to struggling and impoverished nations, even when a good deal of these countries despise us or don't appreciate our efforts. When most countries start wars to crush their enemies and advance their own egocentric causes, we defend the defenseless. We fight for righteousness and protect those sovereign nations who seek freedom and liberty for all.

"It's not where you're from; it's where you're going. It's not what you drive; it's what drives you. It's not what you think; it's what you do. It's not who you were; it's who you become."

- Michael Josephson

Epilogue

When I started writing this book I wanted to give the president the benefit of the doubt, but the more I investigated the matter, the more scandals and misappropriation of American resources and money became painfully evident. Obviously my views are slanted, but for good reason. Even if you disagreed with half the things I outlined in this book, the facts don't lie. Under this president our debt grew out of control, unions grew, the number of IRS agents hired to monitor our activities grew, the size and scope of government grew, government regulations grew, taxes grew, unemployment grew, entitlement programs grew, special interest groups grew, terrorism grew, our mistrust and hatred of one another grew, commodities prices grew, poverty grew out of control, healthcare costs grew and college tuitions grew. If you look at the flip side of the spectrum on what we received back for all of our sacrifice, hard work and putting our faith in the government's broken promises: the middle class shrank, the job market shrank, the number of good jobs available to college graduates shrank, our military shrank, our space program shrank, our influence around the world shrank, the number of doctors and hospitals shrank, the number of people receiving healthcare benefits shrank, the number of small businesses shrank (small businesses make up the heart of our economy), medium household income shrank by 10%, the value of our currency shrank and the growth of our economy shrank to its lowest levels since The Great Depression.

Statistics show that our runaway spending will eventually lead to a decline in our living standards. It's already happening. Currently 43% of all households in this country spend more each year than they earn. How can we think of our children's hope for a better tomorrow if we don't have the resources or the capital to invest in our future? One thing is apparent: our current path is unsustainable. How can we get ahead as a society if we are overtaxed and overburdened with government regulations? How are we going to get ahead if success is frowned upon and our small businesses are constantly besieged by the very government sworn to protect them and their interests?

President Obama's time in office is racked with more scandals and more secrecy than any other sitting president in our history. Why so much secrecy if there's nothing to hide? The reason for the tremendous increase in corruption spewing from Washington nowadays is because we as a society refuse to hold the president's liberal agenda accountable for any wrongdoings. Susan Rice was promoted after continually lying about the Benghazi affair, Kathleen Sebelius never lost her job after wasting hundreds of millions of taxpayer dollars on a healthcare website that is racked with security issues and still doesn't work. Attorney General Eric Holder was never reprimanded after the United States Congress held him in contempt for perjuring himself about Fast & Furious. The federal government continues to insult the intelligence of the American people by pandering to our fears and lying to us on significant issues that directly affect our lives and our pocketbooks. They arrogantly dictate what's good for us without allowing the American people to make decisions that help define their own and their families' future. If we aren't going to hold our government officials accountable for their deceit, then is it any wonder why corruption is running rampant in our government today? We've become disengaged as a society.

The white house has created this false notion of class warfare to pit us against each other polarizing the country. This is an intentional ploy designed to mask the truth and divert attention from the fact that our leader has failed us miserably. The president claims to be a champion of the poor and middle class, but under his tutelage the disparity between classes has risen significantly. Due to this paradigm shift towards an entitlement state, the rich in this country currently hold more of America's wealth than any time over the last half-century. For us to continue to thrive as a country it's essential that we stop disregarding the laws of the constitution that were enacted to protect us. It's the constitution and our Bill of Rights, which created the greatest country the world has ever known. Liberty comes at a price; freedom is not free. If we as a society are complacent in disregarding our birthright, then we have no right to question the eminent direction of our floundering destinies. If we allow ourselves to be used and abused then we have only ourselves to blame when our government takes advantage of us.

What can we do to protect ourselves?

Even though President Obama broke his promise about his presidency becoming the most transparent in our history, we still live in the greatest age of transparency. Knowledge is power and if you want to find "the truth" then the Internet is the single greatest resource for uncovering the facts. First off, a majority of us need to start paying more attention to political issues! A wealth of knowledge is accessible if you are willing to take the time to look into matters. Don't believe me, look for yourselves. The points I outlined in this book are mostly common knowledge and common sense, but I think our society needs reminding. Your survival may depend on how well-informed you are, so arm yourselves. Once you're educated on certain topics, it's important to share this knowledge with others. English author, Edward Bulwer-Lytton once said, *"The pen is mightier than the sword."*

In closing, are there any promises Obama made and kept to those who haven't benefitted his quest for power or helped promote his radical agenda? Are there any commitments he pledged that haven't led to complete and utter betrayal? Where is the relief he guaranteed five years ago? Just remember that a masterful orator doesn't always make an effective leader and a smart man doesn't always designate a moral man. The issue isn't whether you're pro-liberalism or pro-conservatism. It's not whether you're republican, democrat or independent. It has nothing to do with your affiliation to the Tea Party or Libertarians or whether you're far right or far left. It's about which direction you feel the country should follow. Do you want a government that demands control of your life in exchange for handouts or do you want the freedom to control your own destiny? You can't have it both ways. Remember that food stamps and welfare are a death sentence. My mother's favorite catchphrase throughout my entire life is, *"Remember the story of the three little pigs."* For forty years I've been scratching my head asking "what the hell does this mean?" Has my mother lost it or is she smoking crack? When I sat to write this book a light bulb went off in my head and I can honestly say I finally figured out the context of this platitude. If your house isn't built on a sound foundation, the first strong gust of wind that comes along will blow your house down. Likewise, if you don't build a sound future for yourself and your family, if you rely solely on the federal government or a third party to guide your destiny, then your future is in the hands of entities who may not have your best interests at heart. While collecting foods stamps you will probably never escape poverty and you will pass this poverty onto your children. Your "free stuff" comes at a steep price. The sad truth is that you are only borrowing money from you're children and hindering their future earnings potential. You are destroying their chance at the "American Dream!" Statistics don't lie! Don't let the government enslave you.

It's time for America to regain its moral foundation. No matter which direction we decide to take our nation, we as responsible parents and stewards have an obligation to preserve our country for the next generation, just like our parents and grandparent endowed to us. Also, what happens when we finally hand over total control to our government and they no longer need our permission or input on important matters? Do you really think they will continue to give you these handouts, especially without demanding more of your allegiance in return for these reparations? For five years now we are told to give the program a chance. There's an old Chinese proverb that says, *"Fool me once, shame on you, fool me twice, shame on me."* Does anybody still believe that the Obama program is working? Likewise, does anybody still believe that the president's policies will all of a sudden miraculously work over the next three years? I have news for you boys and girls, at the rate our debt is exponentially increasing, a great and prosperous America may not exist in three years.

If you're like me, you're tired of all the excuses and rhetoric coming out of Washington. A large part of the gridlock in Washington today is a result of partisanship. I think the American people are becoming increasingly fed up with the finger-pointing and the blaming on why our problems are growing and nothing is getting resolved. I think it's sad that we have a president who believes, "You can't change Washington from the inside." A real leader doesn't make excuses, he or she works in a bipartisan manner to solve problems. A real leader doesn't blame the opposition for why things don't work, they take responsibility. A real leader steps up. They help others even when it's not in their own best interest. If you think the republicans won't do a better job running the country, at least one thing is apparent, they will butt out of your life. Ohio Governor John Kaisch said it best when asked to define conservatism. He said, *"Conservatism means helping people so that they can learn to help themselves."* Conservatism means that people take responsibility for their own lives and their own future. It means that you alone can determine your success. After all, isn't that the "American Dream? Conservatives believe in a smaller government with less control. They won't overburden the middle class and small businesses with massive governmental regulations and taxation. The fact is that government is very important in helping guide our country but, "big government" is bureaucratic and inefficient. Our Founding Fathers believed strongly in laissez-faire government, which is a French expression for "small government." They adopted our constitution based on this theory. The private sector tend to do a better job running the economy. They produce results quicker and more efficiently because they have a greater stake in the outcome. Politicians tend to promote their own political agendas to help themselves and their constituents while the rest of America suffers. Just look at how the democrats are now scrambling to distance themselves from Obamacare after they overwhelmingly voted for years to support the unpopular bill. They're worried about preserving their own futures and saving their own careers, but at the time they weren't worried about the stress and financial burden the bill was going to impact the middle class. The republican coalition collapsed, fragmenting the party after the debacle with the recent government shut-down geared at defunding Obamacare. They are now backing down on taking a stance against raising the debt ceiling and mollifying sequestration for fear of societal backlash. The Republicans are also afraid for their jobs and are now gun-shy from challenging the president on crucial issues. They are hoping that the highly-dysfunctional Obamacare will collapse on its own without making further waves and causing further damage to their already fragile reputations. Currently half the members of congress are worth more than a million dollars.

It's time for us to stop relying on the government to solve our problems and return to the principles that made us great in the first place—a hard-work ethic, moral values, patience and relying on one another to solve complex problems. This was an ideology once engrained in our very fabric. Collective thinking and sharing allowed us to create and do great things. Like Jeff Daniels said, *"The first step in fixing a problem is first admitting there is a problem."* It's time for America to take back its independence and assume our rightful position as the "top dog" leading the world to a brighter tomorrow. Whether you think Obama is intentionally trying to fundamentally reshape America, or our faltering economy is the result of bad policies is irrelevant—the policies are destroying America regardless. It's time to step up and demand our freedoms back and fight for our liberties. It's the only way we will again reach our full potential.

Albert Einstein once said, *"The definition of insanity is doing the same thing over and over and expecting different results."* Maybe it's time for a change!

BIBILIOGRAPHY

[1] Henderson, David R. July 27, 2012. THE ECONOMICS AND HISTORY OF CRONYISM. Mercatus Center – George Mason University. http://mercatus.org/sites/default/files/Henderson_cronyism_1.1%20final.pdf.

[2] Snyder, C. R.; Lopez, Shane J. (2007). Positive Psychology. Sage Publications, Inc. p. 147. ISBN 0-7619-2633-X.

[3] Anonymous. First Posted: 02/06/2012 5:00 am Updated: 04/07/2012 5:12 am. Food Stamp Fraud Targeted As Election Season Brings Criticism. Huff Post Business. http://www.huffingtonpost.com/2012/02/06/food-stamp-fraud_n_1256684.html.

[4] Benson, Guy. Jun 28, 2012. Flashback Videos: Obama's False Tax Promises. Townhall.com. http://townhall.com/tipsheet/guybenson/2012/06/28/flashback_videos_obamas_tax_lies__plus_romney_reacts.

[5] Bigman, Dan (Managing Editor for Business News). 4/03/2012 @ 2:39PM. John Stossel: Tax The Rich? The Rich Don't Have Enough. Really. Forbes.

http://www.forbes.com/sites/danbigman/2012/0
4/03/john-stossel-tax-the-rich-the-rich-dont-
have-enough-really.

[6] Bigman, Dan (Managing Editor for Business
News). 4/03/2012 @ 2:39PM. John Stossel:
Tax The Rich? The Rich Don't Have Enough.
Really. Forbes.
http://www.forbes.com/sites/danbigman/2012/0
4/03/john-stossel-tax-the-rich-the-rich-dont-
have-enough-really.

[7] Jeffrey, Terence P. December 9, 2013 - 2:21
PM. CBO:Top 40% Paid 106.2% of Income
Taxes; Bottom 40% Paid -9.1%, Got Average
of $18,950 in 'Transfers'. CNSNews.com.
http://cnsnews.com/news/article/terence-p-
jeffrey/cbotop-40-paid-1062-income-taxes-
bottom-40-paid-91-got-average-
18950#sthash.cPId7stQ.dpuf.

[8] Mourdoukoutas, Panos. Contributor.
4/01/2013 @ 7:56PM. What It Takes For China
To Be No 1. Forbes.
http://www.forbes.com/sites/panosmourdoukou
tas/2013/04/01/what-it-takes-for-china-to-be-
no-1.

[9] Berman, Bradley. Retrieved 2013-06-18.
Henrik Fisker Resigns From Fisker
Automotive. The New York Times.

http://wheels.blogs.nytimes.com/2013/03/13/he
nrik-fisker-resigns-from-fisker-
automotive/?_r=0.

[10] MacHaffie, John. September 17th, 2013. The
Complete List of Barack Obama's Scandals,
Misdeeds, Crimes and Blunders. REPUBLIC
NOW - Galactic News.
http://investmentwatchblog.com/the-complete-
list-of-barack-obamas-scandals-misdeeds-
crimes-and-blunders.

[11] MacHaffie, John. September 17th, 2013. The
Complete List of Barack Obama's Scandals,
Misdeeds, Crimes and Blunders. REPUBLIC
NOW - Galactic News.
http://investmentwatchblog.com/the-complete-
list-of-barack-obamas-scandals-misdeeds-
crimes-and-blunders.

[12] Snyder, Jim & Martin Christopher. Sep 12,
2011 12:59 pm ET. Obama Team Backed $535
Million Solyndra Aid as Auditor Warned on
Finances. Bloomberg News.
http://www.bloomberg.com/news/2011-09-
12/obama-team-backed-535-million-solyndra-
aid-as-auditor-warned-on-finances.html.

[13] MacHaffie, John. September 17th, 2013. The
Complete List of Barack Obama's Scandals,
Misdeeds, Crimes and Blunders. REPUBLIC

NOW - Galactic News.
http://investmentwatchblog.com/the-complete-list-of-barack-obamas-scandals-misdeeds-crimes-and-blunders.

[14] Volsky, Igor. October 28, 2013 at 8:59 pm. Here Is What's Wrong With That Story About Obama Knowing That Your Health Care Policy Would Get Cancelled. ThinkProgress.org. http://thinkprogress.org/health/2013/10/28/285 0061/wrong-story-obama-knowing-health-care-policy-cancelled/#.

[15] Kurtz, Stanley. June 7, 2012 4:00 A.M. Obama's Third Party History. The National Review Online. http://www.nationalreview.com/articles/302031 /obamas-third-party-history-stanley-kurtz.

[16] Boyle, Matthew. 30 Oct, 2013. Election Integrity Activists: Obamacare 'Biggest Voter Registration Fraud Scheme in History. Breitbart. http://www.breitbart.com/Big-Government/2013/10/30/Election-Integrity-Activists-Obamacare-Biggest-Voter-Registration-Fraud-Scheme-in-History.

[17] Gattuso, James L. and Katz, Diane. May 1, 2013. Red Tape Rising: Regulation in Obama's First Term. The Heritage Foundation. http://www.heritage.org/research/reports/2013/

05/red-tape-rising-regulation-in-obamas-first-term.

[18]Anonymous. 12/9/2013. Obamacare crashing in model states like California as 70 percent of doctors opt out. Catholic Online, http://www.catholic.org/health/story.php?id=53476.

[19] Bier, Jeryl. Oct 14, 2013, 12:29 P.M. Obamacare Website Source Code: 'No Reasonable Expectation of Privacy. The Weekly Standard. http://www.weeklystandard.com/blogs/obamacare-website-source-code-no-reasonable-expectation-privacy_762489.html.

[20] Chakraborty, Barnini. Published November 06, 2013. Felons could have been hired as ObamaCare 'navigators,' Sebelius tells Senate panel. Fox News. http://www.foxnews.com/politics/2013/11/06/sebelius-back-in-hot-seat-on-capitol-hill-over-rocky-rollout-obamacare.

[21] Weinstein, Jamie. 12:45 AM 11/04/2013. Expert: At least 129 million will 'not be able to keep' health care plan if Obamacare fully implemented. The Dailey Caller. http://dailycaller.com/2013/11/04/expert-at-least-129-million-will-not-be-able-to-keep-health-care-plan-if-obamacare-fully-implemented.

[22] Tagliare, DA. November 12, 2012. Thousands Losing Jobs Due to Obamacare. Godfather Politics. http://godfatherpolitics.com/8034/thousands-losing-jobs-due-to-obamacare.

[23] Saunders, Laura. Nov. 13, 2013 1:15 p.m. ET. More Taxpayers Are Abandoning the U.S. The Wall Street Journal. http://online.wsj.com/news/articles/SB10001424052702304243904579195923107439130

[24] Starnes, Scotty. January 2, 2011. How has Obama Violated the Constitution? Let's Count the Ways. Politically Incorrect Conservative. http://scottystarnes.wordpress.com/2011/01/02/how-has-obama-violated-the-constitution-lets-count-the-ways.

[25] Starnes, Scotty. January 2, 2011. How has Obama Violated the Constitution? Let's Count

the Ways. Politically Incorrect Conservative. http://scottystarnes.wordpress.com/2011/01/02/ how-has-obama-violated-the-constitution-lets-count-the-ways.

[26] Starnes, Scotty. January 2, 2011. How has Obama Violated the Constitution? Let's Count the Ways. Politically Incorrect Conservative. http://scottystarnes.wordpress.com/2011/01/02/ how-has-obama-violated-the-constitution-lets-count-the-ways.

[27] Starnes, Scotty. January 2, 2011. How has Obama Violated the Constitution? Let's Count the Ways. Politically Incorrect Conservative. http://scottystarnes.wordpress.com/2011/01/02/ how-has-obama-violated-the-constitution-lets-count-the-ways.

[28] Helderman, Rosalind S. and Goldstein, Amy. Tuesday, December 14, 2010; 12:49 AM. Federal judge in Va. strikes down part of health-care law. The Washington Post Blog. http://www.washingtonpost.com/wp-dyn/content/article/2010/12/13/AR2010121302 420.html.

[29] MacHaffie, John. September 17th, 2013. The Complete List of Barack Obama's Scandals, Misdeeds, Crimes and Blunders. REPUBLIC NOW - Galactic News.

http://investmentwatchblog.com/the-complete-list-of-barack-obamas-scandals-misdeeds-crimes-and-blunders.

[30] Battle Jordan, Brenda. Friday, March 1, 2013 15:54. The Obama's, I Knew They Had Both Lost Their Law License, But I Didn't Know Why Until I Read This. Before It's News. http://beforeitsnews.com/blogging-citizen-journalism/2013/03/the-obamas-i-knew-they-had-both-lost-their-law-license-but-i-didnt-know-why-until-i-read-this-2445938.html.

[31] Berman, Leo. Wednesday, April 27th, 2011. The hospital listed on Barack Obama's just-publicized long-form birth certificate denies the president was born there. PolitiFact.com from a Texas Tribune article. http://www.politifact.com/texas/statements/2011/apr/27/leo-berman/state-rep-leo-berman-says-kapiolani-medical-center.

[32] Dr. Conspiracy. April 3, 2009. The African Race. Obama Conspiracy Theories. http://www.obamaconspiracy.org/2009/04/the-african-race.

[33] Dahl, Spencer. August 20, 2012. Four Simple Questions. Bend Bugle. http://www.bendbugle.com/2012/08/four-simple-questions/.

[34] Johannson, Penbrook. Thursday, April 12, 2012. Obama Lawyer Admits Forgery but disregards "image" as Indication of Obama's Ineligibility Damage Control. The Tea Party Tribune. http://www.teapartytribune.com/2012/04/13/obama-lawyer-admits-forgery-but-disregards-image-as-indication-of-obamas-ineligibility-damage-control.

[35] Anonymous. May 15, 2013 7:06pm PST. Alabama Supreme Court Reviews Shocking Evidence Obama's Birth Certificate Likely a Forgery. MrConservatice.com. http://www.mrconservative.com/2013/05/16111-alabama-supreme-court-reviews-shocking-evidence-obamas-birth-certificate-likely-a-forgery.

[36] Sundance. October 9, 2013. Spite House - President Stompy Feet Rules Now Deny Military Active Duty Combat "Death Gratuity" Benefit….. The Last Refuge. http://theconservativetreehouse.com/2013/10/09/spite-house-president-stompy-feet-rules-now-deny-military-active-duty-combat-death-gratuity-benefit.

[37] Carafano, James. March 4, 2009 at 9:37 am. Missile Mayhem. The Foundry.

http://blog.heritage.org/2009/03/04/missile-mayhem.

[38] Kuhner T., Jeffrey. Friday, April 16, 2010. Obama bowing to the world. The Washington Times, http://www.washingtontimes.com/news/2010/apr/16/obama-bowing-to-the-world/?page=al.

[39] Dreyfuss, Robert. Tues Nov. 5, 2013 11:13 AM PST. How American Foreign Policy Is Hurting American Power. MotherJones.com. http://www.motherjones.com/politics/2013/11/us-foreign-policy-decrease-power.

[40] Bakr, Amena and Strobel, Warren. Tue Oct 22, 2013 8:27pm EDT. Saudi Arabia warns of shift away from U.S. over Syria, Iran. Reuters.http://www.reuters.com/article/2013/10/22/us-saudi-usa-idUSBRE99L0K120131022.

[41] HJ, Sat Oct 19, 2013 1:15PM GMT. 33 stats national debt is destroying America. PressTV. http://www.presstv.com/detail/2013/10/19/330201/33-stats-national-debt-is-destroying-us.

[42] Snyder, Michael. April 23rd, 2013. America the Fallen: 24 Signs That Our Once Proud Cities Are Turning Into Poverty-Stricken Hellholes. The Economic Collapse. http://theeconomiccollapseblog.com/archives/a

merica-the-fallen-24-signs-that-our-once-proud-cities-are-turning-into-poverty-stricken-hellholes.

[43] Goldcore Bullion and Wealth Management Company. Jan. 22, 2013, 6:12 PM. China Wants to Wean Itself off The Dollar, But Risks Destroying Chinese Wealth. Business Insider. http://www.businessinsider.com/china-to-challenge-us-dollar-reserve-currency-status-2012-10.

[44] Riley, Charles. October 14, 2013: 12:42 PM ET. World chastises U.S. as debt ceiling looms. CNN Money. http://money.cnn.com/2013/10/14/news/economy/debt-ceiling-world.

[45] Ross, Brian. March 13, 2008. Retrieved 2008-03-17. Obama's Pastor: God Damn America, U.S. to Blame for 9/11. ABC News. http://abcnews.go.com/Blotter/DemocraticDebate/story?id=4443788.

[46] Babington, Charles. Retrieved 2008-03-18. Analysis: Obama grabs race issue. Yahoo! News. Associated Press. Dead Link via Wikipedia.

[47] MacHaffie, John. September 17th, 2013. The Complete List of Barack Obama's Scandals,

Misdeeds, Crimes and Blunders. REPUBLIC NOW - Galactic News. http://investmentwatchblog.com/the-complete-list-of-barack-obamas-scandals-misdeeds-crimes-and-blunders.

[48] Hill, Austin. Aug 19, 2012. The American Dream, or the Dreams of Obama's Father? Townhall.com. http://townhall.com/columnists/austinhill/2012/08/19/the_american_dream_or_the_dreams_of_obamas_father/page/full

[49] BQL Editor. October 25th, 2010. How the Liberal Media is Destroying America. Blackquillandink.com. http://blackquillandink.com/?p=9209.

[50] Science and technology in the United States, Wikipedia, http://en.wikipedia.org/wiki/Science_and_technology_in_the_United_States.